Infinispan Data Grid Platform

Making use of data grids for performance and scalability in Enterprise Java, using Infinispan from JBoss

Francesco Marchioni

Manik Surtani

BIRMINGHAM - MUMBAI

Infinispan Data Grid Platform

First published: August 2012

Production Reference: 1070812

Published by Packt Publishing Ltd.
Livery Place
35 Livery Street
Birmingham B3 2PB, UK..

ISBN 978-1-84951-822-2

`www.packtpub.com`

Cover Image by Asher Wishkerman (`a.wishkerman@mpic.de`)

Credits

Authors
Francesco Marchioni
Manik Surtani

Reviewers
Bill Burke
Jonathan Halliday
Mircea Markus
Alan Santos
Galder Zamarreño

Acquisition Editor
Sarah Cullington

Lead Technical Editor
Dayan Hyames

Technical Editor
Merin Jose

Copy Editor
Brandt D'Mello

Project Coordinator
Leena Purkait

Proofreader
Aaron Nash

Indexer
Rekha Nair

Graphics
Valentina D'silva
Manu Joseph

Production Coordinator
Melwyn D'sa

Cover Work
Melwyn D'sa

About the Authors

Francesco Marchioni is a Sun-certified Enterprise Architect, employed for an Italian company based in Rome. He started learning Java in 1997, and since then, he has followed the path to the newest Application Program Interfaces released by Sun. In 2000, he joined the JBoss Community when the application server was running release 2.X.

He has spent many years as a software consultant, where he has envisioned many successful software migrations from vendor platforms to open source products such as JBoss AS, fulfilling the tight budget requirements of current times.

In the past 5 years, he has started authoring technical articles for O'Reilly Media and running an IT portal focused on JBoss products (`http://www.mastertheboss.com`).

In December 2009, he published the title *JBoss AS 5 Development*, which describes how to create and deploy Java Enterprise applications on JBoss AS (`http://www.packtpub.com/jboss-as-5-development/book`).

In December 2010, he published his second title, *JBoss AS 5 Performance Tuning*, which describes how to deliver fast and efficient applications on JBoss AS (`http://www.packtpub.com/jboss-5-performance-tuning/book`).

In December 2011, he published yet another title, *JBoss AS 7 Configuration, Deployment and Administration*, which covers all the aspects of the newest release of the application server (`http://www.packtpub.com/jboss-as-7-configuration-deployment-administration/book`).

I'd like to thank Packt Publishing for offering me another opportunity to write about my favorite application server. I'd also like to thank my family for supporting me during the creation of this book, in particular my father, for teaching me all the tricks of the glorious C-64 when I was a kid.

Manik Surtani is a core research and development engineer at JBoss, a division of Red Hat. He is the founder of the Infinispan project, which he currently leads. He is also the specification lead of JSR 347 (Data Grids for the Java Platform), and represents Red Hat on the Expert Group of JSR 107 (Temporary caching for Java).

His interests lie in cloud and distributed computing, NoSQL and Big Data, autonomous systems, and highly available computing. He has a background in artificial intelligence and neural networks, a field he left behind when he moved from academic circles to the commercial world. Since then, he's been working with Java-related technologies, first for a startup focusing on knowledge management and information exchange, and later for a large London-based consultancy as a tech lead focused on e-commerce applications on large Java EE and peer-to-peer technology.

Manik is a strong proponent of open source development methodologies, ethos, and collaborative processes, and has been involved in open source since his first forays into computing.

About the Reviewers

Mircea Markus joined JBoss's clustering team in 2007 as a core engineer. He has worked on various clustering components, such as JBossCache, PojoCache, and JGoups. He is one of the founders of the Infinispan project, on which he has been concentrating his efforts for the last two years. He is also the founder of project Radargun—a benchmark for framework data grids.

Alan Santos has been involved with the design, implementation, sale, and support of software for 15 years. Currently a product manager at Red Hat, he has previously worked with Object Design and Progress Software, among others, as a product manager for the DataXtend line of business.

Galder Zamarreño Arrizabalaga is a JBoss Core research and development engineer working for Red Hat. In his current role, he's part of the Infinispan project development team, where he's building next-generation, distributed data grid software, based on Java, Scala, and Python. Galder has previously worked with JBoss customers, helping them build highly distributed and massively scalable Application Server clusters based on technologies such as JGroups and JBoss Cache.

Prior to joining Red Hat, Galder worked in the Retail industry, where he was a software developer involved in the development of an EFT sofware switch solution based on JBoss technologies. The love for distributed systems and open source software comes from his days at ESIDE faculty at University of Deusto (Bilbao, Spain), where he obtained a master's degree in Computer Science. Finally, Galder previously spoke in conferences such as GOTO (formerly JAOO), GeeCON, Miracle Open World, SoftShake, Red Hat Summit/JBoss World, and JUDCon.

www.PacktPub.com

Support files, eBooks, discount offers and more

You might want to visit www.PacktPub.com for support files and downloads related to your book.

Did you know that Packt offers eBook versions of every book published, with PDF and ePub files available? You can upgrade to the eBook version at www.PacktPub.com and as a print book customer, you are entitled to a discount on the eBook copy. Get in touch with us at service@packtpub.com for more details.

At www.PacktPub.com, you can also read a collection of free technical articles, sign up for a range of free newsletters and receive exclusive discounts and offers on Packt books and eBooks.

http://PacktLib.PacktPub.com

Do you need instant solutions to your IT questions? PacktLib is Packt's online digital book library. Here, you can access, read and search across Packt's entire library of books.

Why Subscribe?

- Fully searchable across every book published by Packt
- Copy and paste, print and bookmark content
- On demand and accessible via web browser

Free Access for Packt account holders

If you have an account with Packt at www.PacktPub.com, you can use this to access PacktLib today and view nine entirely free books. Simply use your login credentials for immediate access.

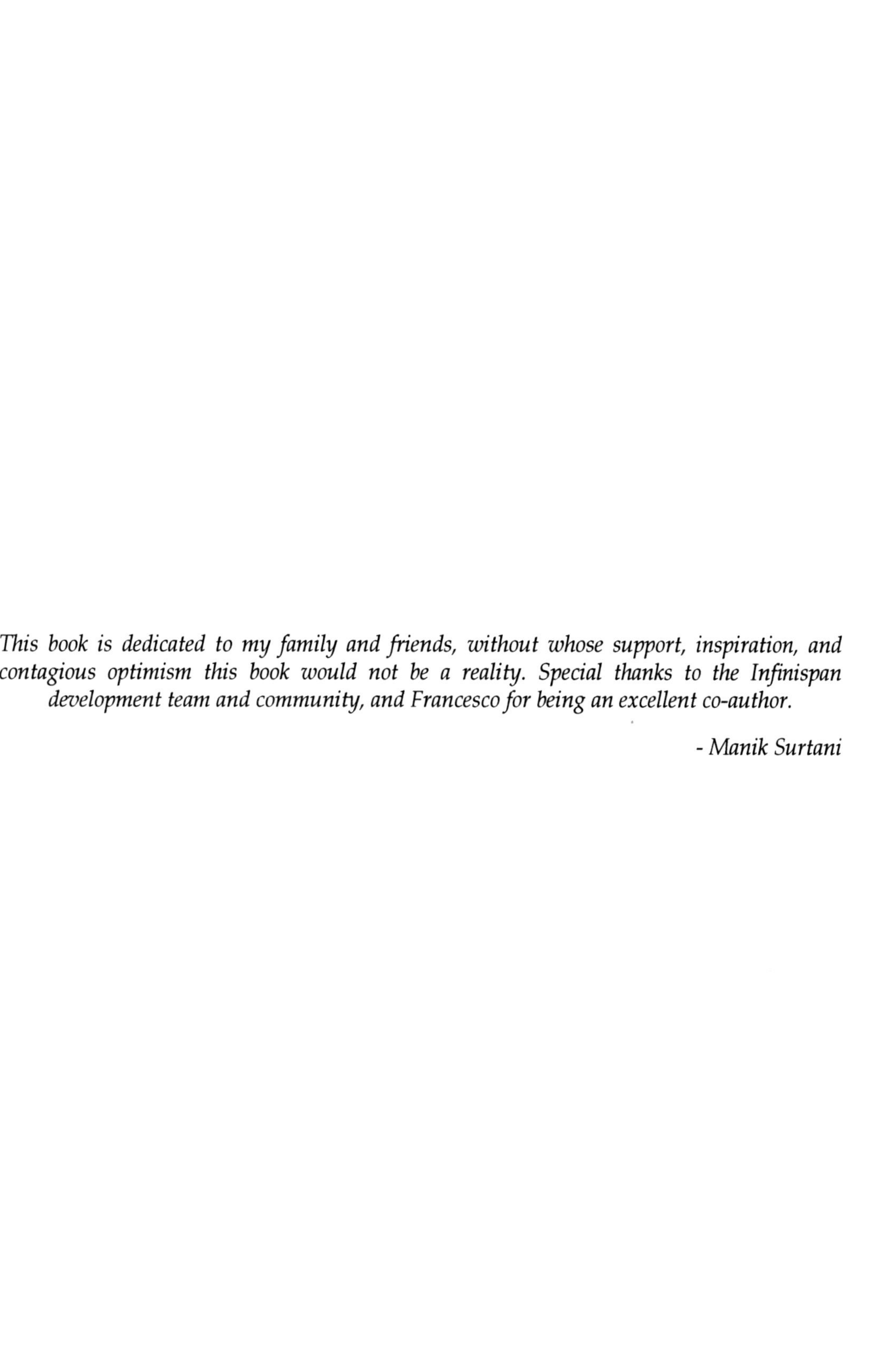

This book is dedicated to my family and friends, without whose support, inspiration, and contagious optimism this book would not be a reality. Special thanks to the Infinispan development team and community, and Francesco for being an excellent co-author.

- Manik Surtani

Table of Contents

Appendix: Infinispan and JBoss AS 7

The Appendix is not present in the book but is available as a free download from the following link: `http://www.packtpub.com/sites/default/files/downloads/8222_Appendix_Final.pdf`.

Preface

In today's competitive business world, Enterprise systems must be able to deliver highly available systems that are able to cope with high transaction volumes with an increasing number of users. Infinispan enables you to do this, as well as share and distribute data among servers, in the most efficient way possible so that you achieve faster response times while trying to avoid single points of failure.

Infinispan Data Grid Platform will teach you the most important concepts for building Enterprise applications that achieve high availability and scalability using data grids. Using Infinispan will give you a decisive competitive advantage over the standard clustering toolkits that are typical in Enterprise today. This is the only book which covers Infinispan, offering detailed instructions for installing, configuring, and effectively using the Infinispan platform. You will learn how to utilize and make the most out of every feature of its API.

Progress from examples of adding, removing, and evicting data from a cache, to more complex scenarios, such as clustering and distributing data more efficiently in the grid. Throughout the book, you will follow a simple example of an API using a ticket booking system, which will help you to learn how to set up robust and scalable Infinispan configurations. You will also see a complete demonstration of integrating the Infinispan data grid platform with JBoss AS 7.

What this book covers

Chapter 1, Installing Infinispan: This chapter will introduce the Infinispan data grid platform by discussing the definition of data grid and its conceptual background. It also shows the installation of the Infinispan platform and a common set of tools that will help us in the development process.

Chapter 2, Using Infinispan Core API: This chapter introduces the core Infinispan API by discussing the two Infinispan operational modes and showing how to interact with the basic Infinispan constructs—the CacheManager interfaces and the Cache API.

Chapter 3, Introducing Infinispan Configuration: In this chapter, we will show both declarative and programmatic approaches with a focus on the basic configuration elements.

Chapter 4, Developing Advanced Configurations: This chapter introduces some advanced topics, such as clustering and transactions that are essential for scalable and reliable Enterprise applications.

Chapter 5, Monitoring Infinispan: This chapter dives into management and monitoring of the Infinispan platform, showing how to collect the relevant information related to Cache Manager and cache objects.

Chapter 6, Infinispan and CDI: This chapter demonstrates using Infinispan with the increasingly popular CDI programming model.

Chapter 7, Advanced Topics: This chapter discusses three of Infinispan's advanced topics—the asynchronous API, the query API, and customizing Infinispan.

Bonus Section—*Appendix A, Infinispan and JBoss AS 7*: In the appendix, we will show how to configure and develop applications using Infinispan API on a JBoss AS 7 server. The Appendix is not present in the book but is available as a free download from the following link: `http://www.packtpub.com/sites/default/files/downloads/8222_Appendix_Final.pdf`.

What you need for this book

OpenJDK 1.6.0 or Sun JDK 1.6.0 or above, and Apache Maven 3.0 or above. Furthermore, a Java Integrated Development Environment (IDE) such as Eclipse is highly recommended.

Who this book is for

This book is for Enterprise developers and architects who want to use a distributed caching and data grid solution. You should have programming knowledge of Java and a general familiarity with concepts such as data caching and clustering.

Conventions

In this book, you will find a number of styles of text that distinguish between different kinds of information. Here are some examples of these styles, and an explanation of their meaning.

Code words in text are shown as follows: "The `stateTransfer` attribute configures how a state is retrieved when a new cache joins the cluster."

A block of code is set as follows:

```
<clustering mode="distribution">
         <sync/>
         <hash
            numOwners="3"
            rehashEnabled="true"
            rehashRpcTimeout="600000"
         />
</clustering>
```

When we wish to draw your attention to a particular part of a code block, the relevant lines or items are set in bold:

```
<transaction
  useEagerLocking="true"
  eagerLockSingleNode="true">
    <recovery enabled="true" />
</transaction>
```

Any command-line input or output is written as follows:

```
mvn --version
Apache Maven 3.0.4 (r1075438; 2011-02-28 18:31:09+0100)
Maven home: C:\apache-maven-3.0.4\bin\..
Java version: 1.6.0, vendor: Sun Microsystems Inc.
Java home: C:\Programmi\Java\jdk1.6.0\jre
Default locale: it_IT, platform encoding: Cp1252
OS name: "windows xp", version: "5.1",
arch: "x86", family: "windows"
```

New terms and **important words** are shown in bold. Words that you see on the screen, in menus or dialog boxes for example, appear in the text like this: "In order to get started, hit the **Start Cache** button, which will instantiate a cache".

Warnings or important notes appear in a box like this.

Tips and tricks appear like this.

Reader feedback

Feedback from our readers is always welcome. Let us know what you think about this book—what you liked or may have disliked. Reader feedback is important for us to develop titles that you really get the most out of.

To send us general feedback, simply send an e-mail to `feedback@packtpub.com`, and mention the book title through the subject of your message.

If there is a topic that you have expertise in and you are interested in either writing or contributing to a book, see our author guide on `www.packtpub.com/authors`.

Customer support

Now that you are the proud owner of a Packt book, we have a number of things to help you to get the most from your purchase.

Downloading the example code

You can download the example code files for all Packt books you have purchased from your account at `http://www.packtpub.com`. If you purchased this book elsewhere, you can visit `http://www.packtpub.com/support` and register to have the files e-mailed directly to you.

The example code for this book is also publicly available in Infinispan's source code repository on GitHub at `http://github.com/infinispan/Infinispan-book`.

Errata

Although we have taken every care to ensure the accuracy of our content, mistakes do happen. If you find a mistake in one of our books—maybe a mistake in the text or the code—we would be grateful if you would report this to us. By doing so, you can save other readers from frustration and help us improve subsequent versions of this book. If you find any errata, please report them by visiting `http://www.packtpub.com/support`, selecting your book, clicking on the **errata submission form** link, and entering the details of your errata. Once your errata are verified, your submission will be accepted and the errata will be uploaded to our website, or added to any list of existing errata, under the Errata section of that title.

Piracy

Piracy of copyright material on the Internet is an ongoing problem across all media. At Packt, we take the protection of our copyright and licenses very seriously. If you come across any illegal copies of our works, in any form, on the Internet, please provide us with the location address or website name immediately so that we can pursue a remedy.

Please contact us at `copyright@packtpub.com` with a link to the suspected pirated material.

We appreciate your help in protecting our authors, and our ability to bring you valuable content.

Questions

You can contact us at `questions@packtpub.com` if you are having a problem with any aspect of the book, and we will do our best to address it.

1
Installing Infinispan

This chapter will introduce the Infinispan data grid platform, starting with two obvious questions: *What is a data grid?* and *Why do we need to learn about it?* We will cover the following topics in detail:

- Data grid definition and its conceptual background
- Installing the Infinispan platform and a common set of tools that will help us in the development process

What is a data grid?

Data growth is one of the biggest challenges faced by today's organizations. It's a fact that the amount of data being used by applications is growing in size, mostly due to the inherent complexity of new Enterprise systems.

In such a scenario, traditional, centralized solutions for storing and retrieving data are not feasible for a set of reasons: first, they are not able to scale as needed, and then they are not suitable to fully address availability and efficiency at such a large scale. For these reasons, many vendors are turning to data grid products, which are a form of middleware that can be used to store a large set of data across distributed applications, over a network.

The most evident benefits of a data grid solution can be summarized in a set of key factors, as follows:

- **Large data set**: Data grids are specifically designed to read and distribute huge sets of data across a set of servers communicating over a network, forming a cluster.
- **Heterogeneity**: The data grid environment is intrinsically heterogeneous both from the software and hardware points of view. This requires a middleware that is able to deal with diverse platforms and storage systems.

- **Scalability**: The data grid is optimized to scale out in environments that produce and use huge amounts of data.

In this picture, we introduce the Infinispan project, which is an open source data grid solution written in Java, providing all the features (and more!) that we have just mentioned. The Infinispan project has grown out of the experiences gained with **JBoss Cache**, the former JBoss AS caching solution; however, it is in no way related to or dependent on JBoss Cache. As a matter of fact, there are several differences between JBoss Cache and Infinispan, the most significant one being the scope. Also, JBoss Cache was focused on being a clustered caching library, whereas Infinispan is a data grid platform, complete with GUI management tooling and the potential to scale to thousands of nodes.

By automatically and dynamically partitioning the data in memory across multiple servers, Infinispan enables continuous data availability and transactional integrity, even in the event of server failure.

The concept of a data grid might be a little difficult to perceive at the beginning because developers are usually accustomed to dealing with simpler entities, such as Hashtables, to cache their data. We will, therefore, start our journey from this simple point of view, and then we will smoothly demystify all the functionalities that make a caching system a data grid.

Introducing Infinispan as a cache

The term cache is generally used to refer to a component that temporarily stores data that is hard to calculate or expensive to retrieve in memory, so that future requests for that data can be served faster. Programmers often employ data structures such as Hashtables or ArrayLists, to maintain in-memory data which is frequently read by your applications.

However, simple `java.util` packages are often too basic to cache your data effectively; and to address this, a **Java Specification Request (JSR-107)** has been created to define a temporary caching API for the Java platform.

Its primary interface is `javax.cache.Cache`, which is similar to `java.util.ConcurrentMap`, with some modifications for distributed environments. In particular, it adds the ability to register, deregister, and list event listeners, and it defines a CacheLoader interface for loading/storing cached data. Cache instances can be retrieved using an appropriate CacheManager, which represents a collection of caches.

Going beyond JSR-107

Although JSR-107 defines some standard APIs for storing and managing data in a local or distributed cache across several nodes, certain APIs specific to a distributed data structure are missing. For example, there is no Future-based asynchronous API.

The JSR-107 specification does not define a mechanism to configure caches. As such, implementations have their own proprietary configuration mechanisms.

With Infinispan, you can either use its simple XML configuration file or define the configuration programmatically. *Chapter 3, Introducing Infinispan Configuration*, and *Chapter 4, Developing Advanced Configurations*, of this book will describe in detail how to configure Infinispan, either in a standalone environment or in a clustered distribution.

As far as replication of data is concerned, it would be worthwhile for a data grid to both full and partial replication of data, in both synchronous and asynchronous manner.

In a fully replicated mode (known simply as **replicated** in Infinispan), all nodes in a cluster hold copies of all entries (if an entry exists on one node, it will also exist on all the other nodes). In a partially replicated mode (known as **distributed** in Infinispan), a fixed number of copies are maintained to provide redundancy and fault tolerance, regardless of cluster size. This is typically far fewer than the number of nodes in the cluster. A partially replicated data grid provides a far greater degree of scalability than a fully replicated one. It is thus the recommended clustering mode in Infinispan.

Finally, **invalidation** is a clustered mode that does not actually share any data at all, but simply aims to remove data that may be stale from remote caches (see *Chapter 4, Developing Advanced Configurations*, for a detailed discussion about cache modes).

Additionally, with Infinispan, you can also use **asynchronous** methods to add/remove entries from the cache by using the non-blocking API; this API combines the advantage of non-blocking calls with the ability to handle communication failures and exceptions.

In conclusion, Infinispan exposes a JSR-107-compatible cache interface in which you can store data, and enhances it by providing additional APIs and features.

Installing the required software

Having introduced the basics of Infinispan, we will now wet our feet by installing the Infinispan platform.

Installing Java SE

The first mandatory requirement is to install a JDK 1.6/JDK 1.7 environment. The Java SE download site can be located at `http://www.oracle.com/technetwork/java/javase/downloads/index.html`.

Choose to download either Java SE 6 or Java SE 7, and install it. If you don't know how to install it, please take a look at the following link:

`http://docs.oracle.com/javase/7/docs/webnotes/install/index.html`

Testing the installation

Once you have completed your installation, run `java -version` to verify that it is correctly installed:

```
C:\Windows>java -version
java version "1.7.0_02"
Java(TM) SE Runtime Environment
  (build 1.7.0_02-b13)
Java HotSpot(TM) Client VM
  (build 22.0-b10, mixed mode, sharing)
```

Installing Maven

The examples contained in this book can be executed from within any development environment of your choice. We will not cover the steps required to install these tools, which in most cases require as little as following a guided wizard procedure.

On the other hand, we would like to describe the installation of Apache Maven, a popular software build and release tool. By using Maven, you will enjoy:

- A standard structure for all your projects
- A centralized and automatic management of dependencies

Maven is distributed in several formats, for your convenience, and can be downloaded from `http://maven.apache.org/download.html`.

Once the download is complete, unzip the distribution archive (for example, `apache-maven-3.0.4-bin.zip`) to the directory in which you wish to install Maven 3.0.4 (or the latest available version), for example `C:\apache-maven-3.0.4`.

Once done, add the `M2_HOME` environment variable to your system, so that it will point to the folder where Maven has been unpacked.

Next, update the `PATH` environment variable by adding the Maven binaries to your system path. For example, on the Windows platform, you should include `%M2_HOME%/bin`, in order to make Maven available in the command line.

Testing the installation

Once you have completed your installation, run `mvn --version`, to verify that Maven has been correctly installed:

```
mvn --version
Apache Maven 3.0.4 (r1075438; 2011-02-28 18:31:09+0100)
Maven home: C:\apache-maven-3.0.4\bin\..
Java version: 1.6.0, vendor: Sun Microsystems Inc.
Java home: C:\Programmi\Java\jdk1.6.0\jre
Default locale: it_IT, platform encoding: Cp1252
OS name: "windows xp", version: "5.1",
  arch: "x86", family: "windows"
```

Installing Infinispan

The Infinispan platform can be freely downloaded from the JBoss community site, `http://www.jboss.org/infinispan/downloads.html`. In this book, we will target the 5.1 release, named **Brahma**.

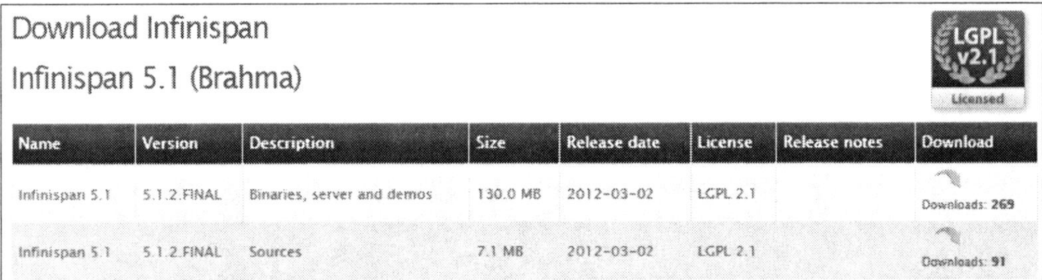
Download Infinispan

Infinispan 5.1 (Brahma)

LGPL v2.1 Licensed

Name	Version	Description	Size	Release date	License	Release notes	Download
Infinispan 5.1	5.1.2.FINAL	Binaries, server and demos	130.0 MB	2012-03-02	LGPL 2.1		Downloads: 269
Infinispan 5.1	5.1.2.FINAL	Sources	7.1 MB	2012-03-02	LGPL 2.1		Downloads: 91

As with most Java libraries, Infinispan does not require running an installer; just unzip the archive in a folder. Let's have a look at its content once you have unpacked the distribution:

```
+---bin
+---doc
+---etc
    +---config-samples
+---lib
+---licenses
+---modules
    +---cachestores
    +---demos
    +---hotrod
    +---hotrod-client
    +---lucene-directory
    +---memcached
    +---query
    +---rhq-plugin
    +---spring
    +---tree
    +---websocket
infinispan-core.jar
```

The `bin` folder contains a few batch scripts that can be used to manage Infinispan.

The most interesting ones are:

- `startServer.bat/startServer.sh`, which can be used to start Infinispan in a standalone JVM process (more about that in the next chapter).
- `importConfig.bat/importConfig.sh`, which can be used to migrate JBoss Cache configurations into the Infinispan configuration file.
- `runGuiDemo.bat/runGuiDemo.sh`, which can be used to test Infinispan's cache using a Java Swing-based demo. We will use it in the next section of this chapter to test the Infinispan installation.

The `doc` folder contains the Javadocs API documentation for Infinispan.

The `etc` directory contains the XML schemas for the Infinispan configuration file (`infinispan-5.1.xsd`) along with some sample configuration files.

The `lib` folder contains some additional libraries that need to be on your `classpath` (or packaged with your deployment), along with the main library `infinispan-core.jar`, which can be located at the root of the Infinispan archive.

The `modules` directory contains a number of optional modules (such as the Infinispan query module or REST interface). In order to use them, you will need to add the module's JAR file and all of its dependencies (`modules/MODULE_NAME/lib`) to be on your `classpath`, in addition to Infinispan's JARs mentioned earlier.

Finally, the `licenses` directory contains the licenses for some of the other libraries shipped with the distribution and not covered by the LGPL-2.1 license, such as Apache's Lucene libraries.

Extending Infinispan with its additional modules

Most Infinispan functionalities are provided by the **core library** (`infinispan-core.jar`), which is placed at the root of the distribution. Infinispan, however, has a highly extensible architecture, making it easy to plug in additional extensions. By default, the Infinispan distribution ships with a set of additional modules, which are contained in the `modules` folder of the distribution.

The `cacheStore` module, for example, allows Infinispan to store cached data in a persistent location, such as a shared JDBC database, a local filesystem, among others.

The `hotrod` folder contains a server module featuring a custom binary protocol for communicating with a remote Infinispan cluster.

The **hotrod** wire protocol is designed to enable faster client/server interactions and also allows clients to make more intelligent decisions with regards to load balancing, failover, and even data location operations. The next chapter shows an example of a remote client connecting to an Infinispan server, using the hotrod protocol.

Another server endpoint is found in the `memcached` directory. This allows memcached clients to talk to one or more Infinispan servers using the memcached wire protocol.

The memcached wire protocol was developed as a means to connect to the simple, non-clustered memcached caching daemon. As a simple cache, memcached was designed to speed up access to dynamic database-driven websites by caching data and objects in memory, to reduce the number of times an external data source must be read. It is currently adopted in most of the popular social networking sites, such as Facebook or Twitter.

Next, the `lucene-directory` folder contains a highly scalable Apache Lucene directory implementation that can be used to provide reliable index sharing across the cluster.

The `query` module, also making use of Apache Lucene in combination with Hibernate Search, adds querying capabilities to Infinispan. This module allows users to search for stored data without access to a specific key. So, you can now search for your data based on their attributes (for example, the tickets sold in one country).

The `rhq-plugin` directory contains libraries that can be used to manage multiple Infinispan instances using the the web-based, open source RHQ management platform. Thanks to RHQ's agent and auto-discovery capabilities, monitoring both CacheManager and Cache instances is a very simple task (see *Chapter 5, Monitoring Infinispan,* for more information about managing Infinispan with RHQ agent).

Another addition can be located in the `spring` folder. The libraries contained in this folder allow you to use Infinispan as a Spring Cache API instead of the default implementations, which ship with Spring.

Finally, the `tree` folder contains Infinispan's tree API module, which offers clients the possibility of storing data using a hierarchical (tree-like) structured API. This API is similar to the one provided by JBoss Cache, hence the tree module is perfect for those users wanting to migrate their applications from JBoss Cache to Infinispan.

If you feel more adventurous, you can even develop your own extensions to let you extend Infinispan beyond its core use case. See this resource for more information about it:

`https://docs.jboss.org/author/display/ISPN/Extending+Infinispan`

Testing the installation with the GUI demo

As we mentioned, Infinispan ships with a GUI demo that can be used to test its basic caching functionalities, either as a standalone server or as a clustered server. We will use it to test our environment without the need to write code:

1. Move into the `bin` folder and execute the `runGuiDemo.bat/runGuiDemo.sh` script.

Please note that this GUI demo uses the configuration file named `gui-demo-cache-config.xml`, contained in `infinispan-gui-demo.jar`. You can switch to another configuration file by passing the `-Dinfinispan.configuration.file` parameter to the `start demo` script.

2. Once launched, the GUI will display the following frame:

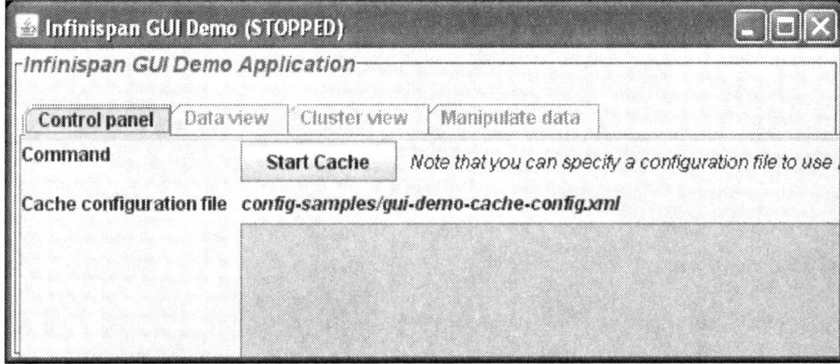

3. In order to get started, hit the **Start Cache** button, which will instantiate a cache.
4. Move to the **Manipulate data** tab. In this tab, you can perform CRUD operations on the cache, including generating bulk random inserts. In the following example, we are adding a sample entry in the cache by filling the **Key** and **Value** textboxes and hitting the **Go** button:

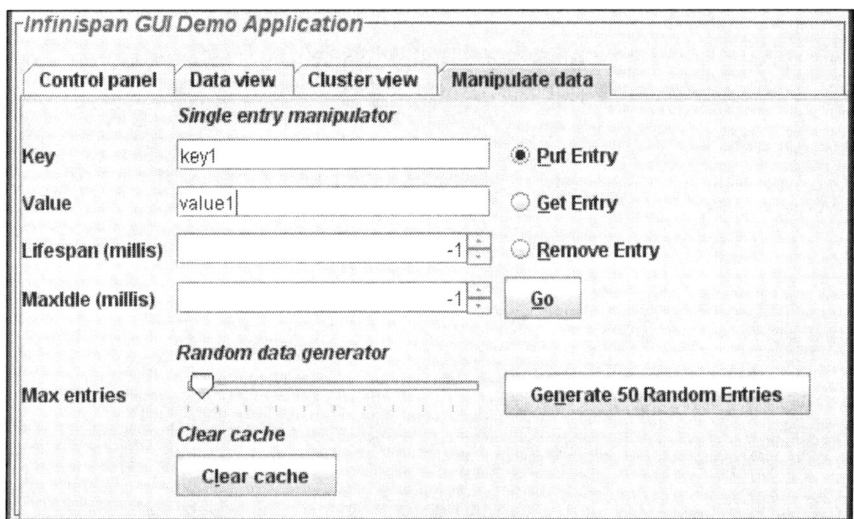

5. Once added, the Demo GUI will switch automatically to the **Data view** tab, which will display the list of entries contained in the cache.

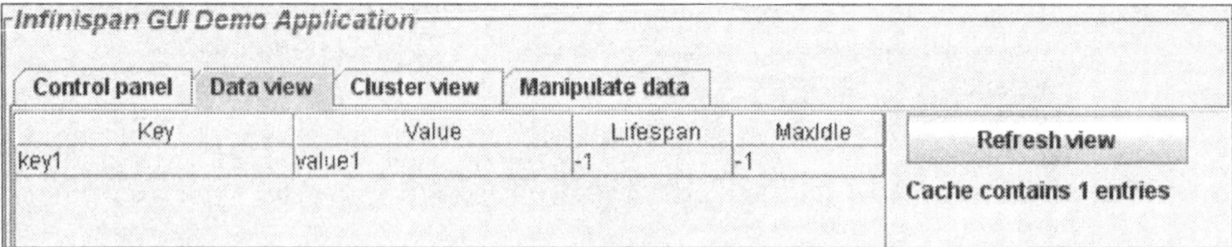

The Infinispan GUI demo application is a simple but effective example application that starts a standalone Infinispan cache and is also able to distribute the cache data across a cluster of JVMs. You can check out the cluster functionalities by starting several demo GUIs and verifying that data is distributed across the other JVMs.

Summary

In this chapter, we have described the requirements for a highly available and fast access to data in today's Enterprise class systems, and the common solution involving in-memory data grids.

Although JSR-107 sets some standards for distributed cached data, it is likely that Enterprise services will need a much more complete approach, often resorting to vendor-specific extensions that reside outside the standard JSR-107 APIs.

Infinispan already provides all of what JSR-107 requires, and much more, by using its core libraries and the additional modules that are contained in the `modules` folder of the platform distribution.

Next, we covered how to install Infinispan and a set of tools (J2SE and Maven) that are needed to develop applications with this platform.

In the next chapter, we will familiarize ourselves with Infinispan API by running our first code samples, which will grow more complex as we go through the other chapters of this book.

2
Using Infinispan Core API

In the first chapter of this book, we had a short overview of the Infinispan platform. That was to whet your appetite—now let's look at writing some codes using this exciting new data grid platform. In this chapter, we will introduce the core Infinispan API by covering the following topics:

- At first, we will look at the two modes of operation in which Infinispan can be used
- In the next section, we will start learning how to interact with the basic Infinispan constructs—the CacheManager interfaces and the Cache API

Infinispan operational modes

There are basically two ways in which you can interact with Infinispan:

- **Embedded mode**: This is when you start Infinispan within the same JVM as your applications (for example, the applications deployed on JBoss Application Server are able to interact with an Infinispan instance that is embedded in the application server)
- **Client-server mode**: This is when you start a remote Infinispan instance and connect to it using a variety of different protocols

There is no recommended way to run Infinispan. As it depends on a number of factors usually connected with the requirements of your applications, it may vary from case to case. In the next sections, we will illustrate both approaches, showing the pros and cons of each solution, so you will be able to choose the solution that is best for you.

Running Infinispan in embedded mode

This operational mode is usually adopted when you want to run your code in the same JVM that hosts an Infinispan instance. If your application is deployed in JBoss Application Server (version 7 and above), you already have an Infinispan instance available for use.

Starting a cache in embedded mode is extremely simple and only requires the mediation of the **CacheManager** interface, which is the primary mechanism used for retrieving a cache instance. For example, here's how you can start a local, non-clustered cache instance:

```
DefaultCacheManager m = new DefaultCacheManager();
Cache<String, String> cache = m.getCache();
```

Starting an instance with more than just the defaults, such as enabling cluster-awareness capable of detecting neighboring instances on the same local area network and sharing a state between them, is also quite simple. Here is an example that specifies a configuration XML file, containing details of your cache configuration:

```
String configFile = "/path/to/config.xml";
DefaultCacheManager m = new DefaultCacheManager(configFile);
Cache<String, String> cache = m.getCache();
```

We will learn more about Infinispan configuration in the next chapter; for the moment, you should be aware that, once started in a clustered mode, the node instances are able to find each other, making up a data grid, and sharing and distributing data across the grid.

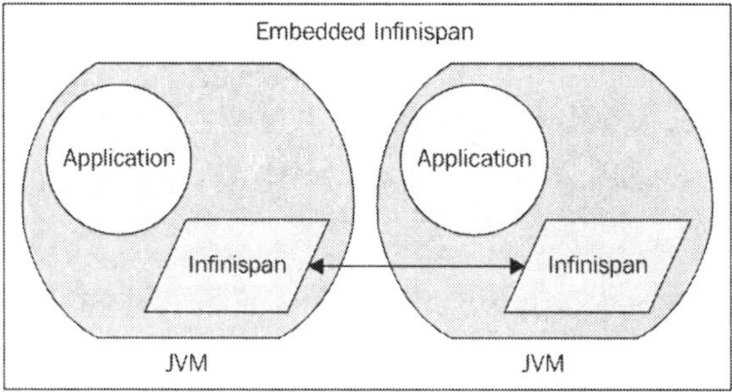

Embedded mode is easy to set up and requires little configuration effort. This mode is suggested when Infinispan is used as a cache —local or distributed— instead of a costly data store; for example, when caching Hibernate entities (the Hibernate "second level cache"). This is also recommended when you wish to cluster-enable your application by delegating state management to Infinispan.

On the other hand, when Infinispan data grid instances are deployed, embedded alongside your application code, starting and stopping these instances can be a slow process due to state transfer, discovery, and other related tasks that Infinispan performs, particularly when the data sets are large.

Moving your data grid to a separate, and dedicated tier provides faster and more predictable server start/stop times, controlled outages, better tuning of hardware and JVMs, as well as the ability to share the data grid across multiple applications—all the ideal features for modern cloud-based deployments, where elasticity and flexibility in your application tier is important.

Running Infinispan in client-server mode

The client-server mode requires, of course, setting up the infrastructure to house Infinispan as a server, and then connecting to it from a variety of different clients. A typical use case can be if you are accessing Infinispan from a non-Java environment, such as Jython, JRuby, Scala, or Groovy, by simply adding the necessary client libraries on the `classpath` variable.

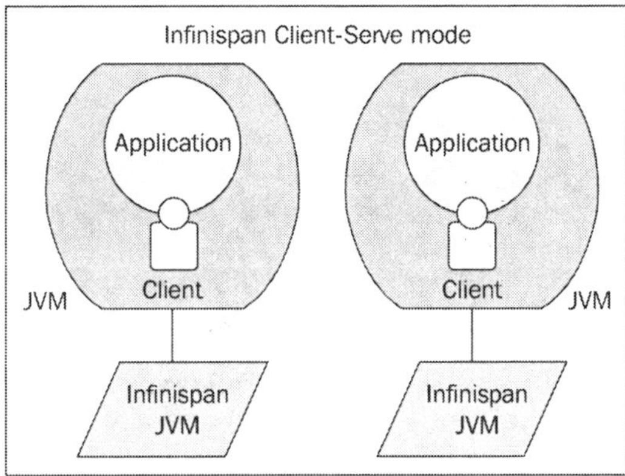

Starting an Infinispan server is fairly straightforward. All you need to do is use the `startServer` script located in the `bin` folder of your distribution. For example:

```
C:\infinispan-5.1.2.FINAL\bin>startServer.bat -r hotrod
```

The script takes in a set of switches to control the endpoint behaviour. The only mandatory parameter is the communication protocol, which can be either `memcached` or `hotrod`. In addition to these two protocols, it's also possible to interact with the Infinispan server via a RESTful API over HTTP. Before diving into the platform API, let's learn the basics of each available protocol.

The memcached protocol

The memcached option causes the Infinispan server endpoint to use the **memcached text wire** protocol. This wire protocol was originally adopted by Infinispan to make use of the ubiquity of memcached, and the availability of many open source client libraries, available for almost any platform. All of the benefits of using Infinispan—including forming a cluster of servers, sharing state to provide greater scalability, high availability and sheer capacity—can be experienced over this protocol. The main weak point of this protocol is the lack of dynamicity. Because of this limitation, when one node of the cluster fails, even if its data is preserved, you need to manually update the list of server nodes on your clients.

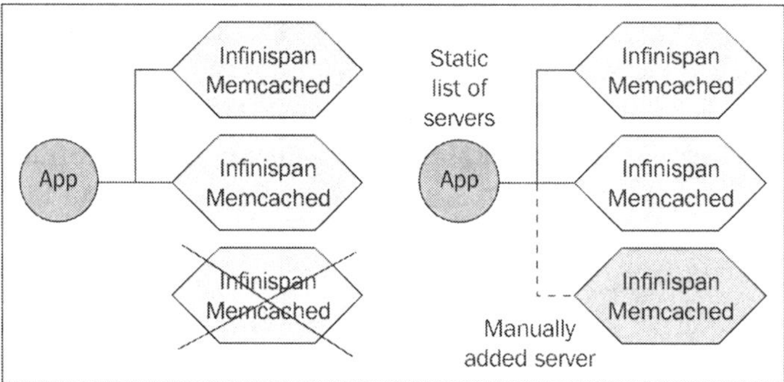

Memcached is a simple yet powerful option, however, for more dynamic client configuration, you might consider the **Hot Rod** protocol as a valid alternative.

The Hot Rod protocol

Hot Rod is an an open, community-developed binary wire protocol designed for Infinispan. The protocol is platform-independent and clients exist for Java, C#, Python and Ruby—with more being contributed regularly. If ease of configuration and maintenance is your main consideration, this should be your first option because the protocol allows for clients to be built to take advantage of dynamic load balancing and failover. This means that Hot Rod clients can *automatically* detect changes in the topology of Hot Rod servers, as long as these are clustered. Thus, when new nodes join or leave the cluster, clients update their Hot Rod server topology view.

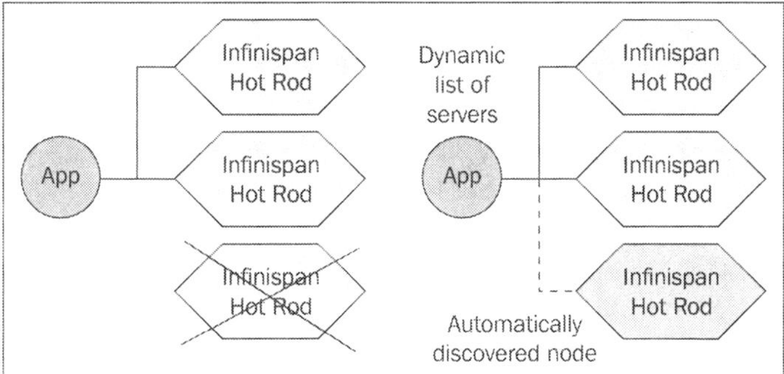

Furthermore, the Hot Rod wire protocol allows for clients to perform smart routing. This technique—which involves the sharing of a consistent hash algorithm between the server nodes and clients—results in minimizing network hops in locating data, translating to faster reads and writes.

Infinispan REST interface

Besides the two basic communication protocols (memcached and Hot Rod), it is also possible to interact with your Infinispan using a RESTful web interface. This kind of interface is delivered as a **Web application ARchive** (**WAR**) file, which can be deployed in any Servlet container. It is a valid option for non-Java clients, or clients where you need to use HTTP as the transport mechanism for caching/data grid needs. See the product documentation at `https://docs.jboss.org/author/display/ISPN/Infinispan+REST+Server`, for more information about it.

Using the Hot Rod Java client

Connecting to a remote Infinispan server can be done using the Hot Rod Java client, located in the `modules` folder of your distribution.

You would need to add the `infinispan-client-hotrod.jar` library, which is located in the `modules/hotrod-client` folder, and its dependencies, which are located in the `lib` subfolder, to your `classpath`.

Here's a sample Hot Rod client that connects to a remote cache (located on the host `192.168.10.1`) using the `org.infinispan.client.hotrod.RemoteCacheManager` interface:

```
RemoteCacheManager rcm = new RemoteCacheManager("192.168.10.1");
RemoteCache rc = rcm.getCache();
String key = "hello";
// Storing data
rc.put(key, "world");
// Retrieving data
System.out.printf("Value of key %s is %s", key, rc.get(key));
```

Once an instance of the `RemoteCacheManager` class is created, we will be able to retrieve a RemoteCache instance, which provides a connection to an Infinispan cluster using the Hot Rod wire protocol.

Learning the Infinispan API

Having introduced some basic concepts of the Infinispan platform, we will now learn how to use the core API to store, retrieve, and remove data in it.

The core interface of Infinispan is `org.infinispan.Cache`, which extends the `java.util.concurrent.ConcurrentMap`, providing a highly concurrent and optionally distributed data structure. Compared with the ConcurrentMap interface, the Infinispan Cache has a lot of additional features, such as:

- Eviction and expiration support to prevent `OutOfMemoryErrors`
- JTA transaction compatibility
- Event notification via the Listeners
- Persistence of entries to a cache store, to maintain copies that would withstand server failure or restarts

For the purpose of exploring the APIs, we will now construct a simple example that creates a cache to store in-memory data for a ticket booking system.

Creating your first project

In order to run your first example, you can launch your favorite IDE and create a new Java project:

1. Set up your project libraries to include the Infinispan core library (`infinispan-core.jar`), which is located at the root of your distribution, and the dependencies, which are placed in the `lib` folder.

[You are advised to create a new **User Library**, which contains a set of all the required JAR files, as shown by the following screenshot taken from the Eclipse environment.]

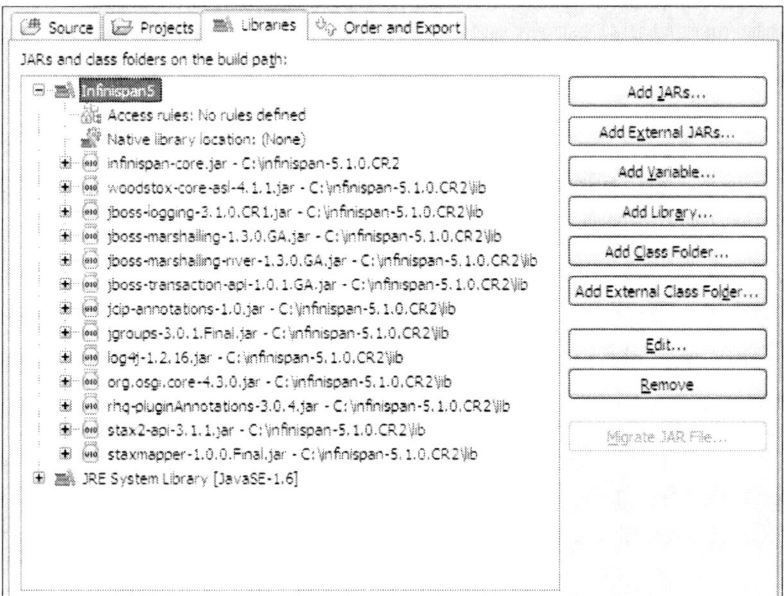

2. Now add a Java class, named `SimpleCache`, to your project:

```
public class SimpleCache {

  public void start(){
    DefaultCacheManager manager =
      new DefaultCacheManager();
    Cache<Integer, Ticket> cache =
      manager.getCache();
    String command = "";
    int ticketid = 1;

    IOUtils.dumpWelcomeMessage();

    while (true){
```

```
            command = IOUtils.readLine("> ");
            if (command.equals("book")) {
              String name =
                IOUtils.readLine("Enter name ");
              String show =
                IOUtils.readLine("Enter show ");

              Ticket ticket = new Ticket(name,show);
              cache.put(ticketid, ticket);
              log("Booked ticket "+ticket);
              ticketid++;
            }
            else if (command.equals("pay")) {
              Integer id = new Integer
                (IOUtils.readLine("Enter ticketid "));
              Ticket ticket = cache.remove(id);
              log("Checked out ticket "+ticket);
            }
            else if (command.equals("list")) {
              Set <Integer> set = cache.keySet();
              for (Integer ticket: set) {
                log(cache.get(ticket));
              }
            }
            else if (command.equals("quit")) {
              cache.stop();
              log("Bye");
              break;
            }
            else {
              log("Unknown command "+command);
              IOUtils.dumpWelcomeMessage();
            }
          }

        }
        public static void main(String[] args) {
          new SimpleCache().start();
        }
      }
```

As you can see, our first example resembles a simple Java caching system. The main difference from a standard Java `Map` object is that the cache object is built from the `DefaultCacheManager` factory, inferring the type `Integer` for the cache key and the associated `Ticket` class.

(For the sake of brevity, we haven't included the `Ticket` class, which is a simple POJO, and `IOUtils`, which is a utility class used for reading input from the keyboard).

Downloading the example code

You can download the sample code files for all Packt books you have purchased from your account at `http://www.packtpub.com`. If you purchased this book elsewhere, you can visit `http://www.packtpub.com/support` and register to have the files e-mailed directly to you.

The sample code for this book is also available at GitHub social repository, at the address: `https://github.com/infinispan/Infinispan-book`.

Controlling the size of your data store

In our first example, data that is added to the cache is immortal, which means that, unless the user manually removes it, it's going to stay there forever. Storing data in memory provides the fastest data access, and thus it is commonly used to improve the performance of distributed applications.

However, more often than not, applications need to ensure that the total amount of data placed into the data grid does not exceed some predetermined amount or does not remain in the memory forever. When using a plain Java `Map` object, you have no option but to manually remove the entries that are not needed anymore.

However, when using Infinispan, you have two mechanisms out-of-the-box, to control memory usage: **eviction** and **expiration**. Let's look at both of them in detail.

Data eviction

Eviction is used to prevent your application from running out of memory. You can evict data from your cache either programmatically or via the configuration file. Generally, eviction is used in conjunction with passivation, as the data which is evicted might be required by the application in the future (we will learn how to configure passivation in the next chapter, which is about Infinispan configuration).

The key configuration parameter used by the eviction thread is `maxEntries`, which represents the maximum number of entries that are allowed in memory:

```
<eviction strategy="LRU" maxEntries="2000"/>
```

The eviction strategy can be chosen between a set of different options, as follows:

Eviction strategy	Description
NONE	The eviction thread will be disabled.
UNORDERED	The data is kept in un-ordered style, thus entries selected for eviction are chosen in an indeterminate fashion.
LRU	Entries are selected for eviction based on the **Least Recently Used** (**LRU**) pattern.
LIRS	Default eviction strategy. A variation of the LRU algorithm that addresses weak access locality shortcomings of LRU. For more information about it, please refer to `http://dl.acm.org/citation.cfm?id=511334.511340`.

Eviction can also be triggered programmatically, using the `evict` method of the Cache interface:

```
Cache cache = manager.getCache();
Ticket ticket = new Ticket(name,show);
cache.put(ticketid, ticket);
cache.evict(ticketid);
```

Data expiration

This feature allows you to attach lifespan and/or maximum idle times to entries. Entries that exceed these times are treated as invalid and are removed. When entries expire, they are not passivated like evicted entries, even if passivation is enabled. As a matter of fact, expired entries are meant to be useless for your application; that's why they are removed **globally** from memory, cache stores, and cluster-wide.

In the following example, we have updated our `Ticket` code example by setting a lifespan of `60` seconds on the entries stored:

```
Ticket ticket = new Ticket(name,show);
cache.put(ticketid, ticket, 60, TimeUnit.SECONDS);
```

This will obviously mean that ticket bookings will expire in 60 seconds, thus you need to check them out by that time.

Data expiration can also be triggered when entries are idle for an amount of time. For example, in the following code, the entry will expire 30 seconds after it is last accessed:

```
cache.put(ticketid, ticket, -1,
  TimeUnit.SECONDS, 30, TimeUnit.SECONDS);
```

Note that, in this example, we have attached a `-1` value to the entry lifespan. This means that the entry will expire on the condition that it has been idle for 30 seconds, but not on its lifespan. You can, however, mix and match the two policies to define both a lifespan as well as a maximum idle time.

Using listeners

Infinispan ships with a rich event notification system. This mechanism allows you to register listeners on some objects and receive notifications when certain events happen. Listeners can be attached to both Cache and Cache Manager, to listen for cache-and cache manager-level events.

When used at cache-level, listeners will be notified of events such as adding or removing entries from the cache. On the other hand, when attached to the cache manager, available events include ones related to the startup/shutdown of the cache or topology change in the cluster.

Creating listeners are quite simple as they are just POJO instances that are marked with the `@org.infinispan.notifications.Listener` annotation.

The following example shows a Listener class that is able to intercept both cache events and cache manager-related events:

```
@Listener
public class SimpleListener {
  @CacheEntryCreated
     public void dataAdded
    (CacheEntryCreatedEvent event) {
       if (event.isPre()) {
         System.out.println
        ("Going to add new entry " +
        event.getKey() + " created in the cache");
       }
       else {
         System.out.println("Added new entry "
        + event.getKey() + " to the cache");
       }
    }
  @CacheEntryRemoved
     public void dataRemoved
    (CacheEntryRemovedEvent event) {
       if (event.isPre()) {
         System.out.println
        ("Going to remove entry " +
        event.getKey() + " created in the cache");
    }
```

```
        else {
          System.out.println("Removed entry " +
        event.getKey() + " from the cache");
        }

      }
    @CacheStarted
      public void cacheStarted
     (CacheStartedEvent event) {
        System.out.println("Cache Started");
      }
    @CacheStopped
      public void cacheStopped
     (CacheStoppedEvent event) {
        System.out.println("Cache Stopped");
      }
}
```

As you can see, each method should be annotated with the event it is interested in. Listener methods annotated with these events must be `public`, return a `void`, and take in a single parameter representing the event type.

For example, the method annotated with `@org.infinispan.notifications.cachelistener.annotation.CacheEntryCreated` annotation will be invoked when a new entry is added to the cache, while the corresponding method annotated with `@org.infinispan.notifications.cachelistener.annotation.CacheEntryRemoved` will be invoked, and an entry will be removed from the cache.

Please note that cache-related events are triggered twice by Infinispan, once **before** and once **after** the event happens. You can use the `isPre` method on the event instance to detect which of the two events has taken place.

The other two methods annotated with, `@org.infinispan.notifications.cachemanagerlistener.annotation.CacheStarted` and `@org.infinispan.notifications.cachemanagerlistener.annotation.CacheStopped`, are invoked when starting and stopping the cache:

```
SimpleListener listener =
  new SimpleListener();
DefaultCacheManager manager =
  new DefaultCacheManager();
manager.addListener(listener);
Cache<Integer, Ticket>
  cache = m.getCache();
cache.addListener(listener);
```

The following table describes the annotations that can be added to intercept the cache-and cache manager-related events:

Annotation	Description
`CacheStarted`	A cache was started
`CacheStopped`	A cache was stopped
`CacheEntryModified`	A cache entry was modified
`CacheEntryCreated`	A cache entry was created
`CacheEntryRemoved`	A cache entry was removed
`CacheEntryVisited`	A cache entry was visited
`CacheEntryLoaded`	A cache entry was loaded
`CacheEntriesEvicted`	A cache entry was evicted
`CacheEntryActivated`	A cache entry was activated
`CacheEntryPassivated`	A cache entry was passivated
`ViewChanged`	A view change event was detected
`TransactionRegistered`	The cache has joined a transaction
`TransactionCompleted`	The cache has completed its participation in a transaction
`CacheEntryInvalidated`	A cache entry was invalidated by a remote cache (only if cache mode is `INVALIDATION_SYNC` or `INVALIDATION_ASYNC`)

Listeners and synchronicity

Notifications are, by default, dispatched synchronously. That is, the call-back that your listener receives happens on the same thread that causes the event.

This means that, if your listener performs tasks that could be slow, the original caller's thread that triggered the event will block until your listener completes.

This side effect can be undesirable for certain applications, so the general recommendation is that your listener implementations must not perform any long-running tasks or tasks that could block another thread.

If you still need to perform such tasks, you can alternatively annotate your listener with the following:

```
@Listener(sync = false)
public class SimpleListener {
. . . .
}
```

The `sync = false` attribute will force an asynchronous dispatch of notifications for this listener. This means that the notifications will be invoked by a separate thread pool and won't block the original caller's thread that triggered the event.

Infinispan and transactions

One more feature of Infinispan is **transaction** support. Infinispan is an XA resource that is compatible with any JTA-compliant transaction manager.

A **transaction manager** is responsible for making the final decision to either commit or roll back any distributed transaction. A commit decision should lead to a successful transaction; rollback leaves the data in the system unaltered.

When transactions are enabled, Infinispan operations performed on the cache object will join any ongoing distributed transaction. Infinispan registers a synchronization with the transaction manager, so it gets a callback to tell it when to flush changes to the data container. As shown in the following screenshot, when a cache is started, it registers itself with the `TransactionManager (1)`:

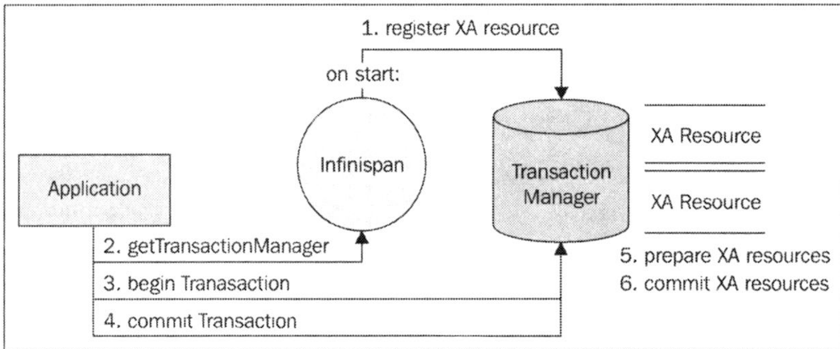

When you need to demarcate a JTA transaction, your application will use `TransactionManager(2)` (usually by obtaining UserTransaction from JNDI, if using a Java EE environment) and begin `Transaction(3)`, so that the current transaction is associated with the running thread.

Once you are done with your transaction, you will issue either a commit or a rollback, and this is propagated up to `TransactionManager`, which will prepare the XA resources for commit or rollback.

In terms of code, you just need to demarcate your transaction with `begin()` and `commit()/rollback()`, at the end of your transaction. In the following sample code, the **UserTransaction** interface is used to demarcate your transaction boundaries, within which some data is added into the cache:

```
@Resource
private UserTransaction utx;

public void executeTransaction() {
   CacheManager manager = new DefaultCacheManager();
   Cache cache = manager.getCache();

   utx.begin();
   cache.put(1, ticket);
   utx.commit();
}
```

One important thing to note is that the keys that are a part of the transaction are locked for writes, although you can still read the keys in another concurrent transaction. In the former example, the entry under key `1`, which is associated with a ticket, will be locked, thus preventing a concurrent transaction from acquiring a concurrent on the same key.

Once the transaction associated with the current thread has completed, the entry under key `1` will be unlocked and made available for update by other transactions.

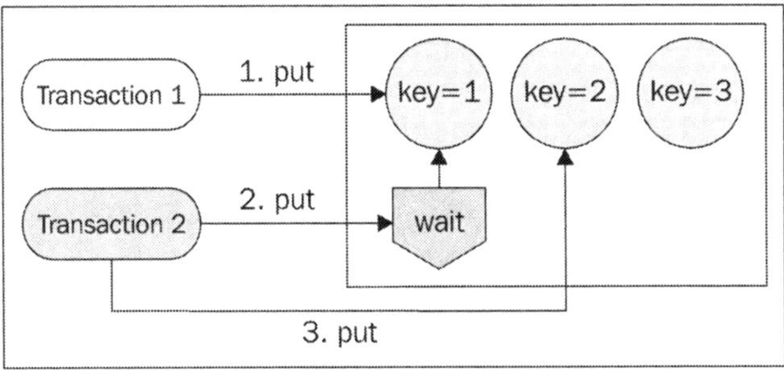

When working on a cluster of nodes, by default, Infinispan acquires cluster locks lazily, that is, at commit time. This is kind of concurrency control is also known as **optimistic locking**, and it assumes that multiple transactions can complete without affecting each other and that, therefore, transactions can proceed without locking the data resources that they affect until the transaction is ready to complete.

This concurrency control has a significant performance impact, as the number of RPC calls is reduced, which is a major overhead for applications using distributed transactions. You will learn more about this in *Chapter 4*, which is about clustering.

Running the sample application with Maven

The examples that we have introduced can be also tested with as little as a command shell and the Apache Maven tool. In the first chapter of this book, we described how to get started with Maven by installing the framework on your PC. Now, it's time to learn how to use it to test drive your examples.

Now unpack the examples zip files in a folder of your choice, and dig into the root of it:

```
C:\infinispan-Infinispan-book-5733128>dir
Directory di C:\infinispan-Infinispan-book
19/06/2012  19.19    <DIR>           chapter2
19/06/2012  19.19    <DIR>           chapter3
19/06/2012  19.26    <DIR>           chapter4
23/05/2012  02.11    <DIR>           chapter5
19/06/2012  20.39    <DIR>           chapter6
19/06/2012  19.27    <DIR>           chapter7
19/06/2012  19.18    <DIR>           common
23/05/2012  02.11              3.908 pom.xml
23/05/2012  02.11              1.855 README.md
                3 File         5.998 byte
```

As you can see, one of the most important additions is the `pom.xml` file, which is the core of a project's configuration in Maven. It is a single configuration file that contains the majority of the information required to build a project in just the way you want. To learn more about Maven and the `pom.xml` file, visit the Apache Maven documentation on (`http://maven.apache.org`). For our purposes, we will just highlight the section that configures the required dependencies, so that you are able to compile and test your classes:

```
<properties>
   <version.infinispan>5.1.5.FINAL</version.infinispan>
</properties>
 . . . . .
<dependencies>
   <dependency>
      <groupId>org.infinispan</groupId>
      <artifactId>infinispan-core</artifactId>
      <version>${version.infinispan}</version>
   </dependency>
</dependencies>
```

As you can see in the generated `pom.xml` file, we are linking to release 5.1.5.FINAL of Infinispan. It is generally recommended to always use the latest stable release of Infinispan, so you might want to replace the highlighted line with the following:

```
<version>LATEST</version>
```

Ok, now we will compile the project by issuing the following command:

```
C:\infinispan-Infinispan-book>mvn compile
[INFO] Scanning for projects...
[INFO]
[INFO] ------------------------------------------------------------------
------[INFO] Building A sample project using Infinispan 5.1
[INFO]
[INFO] Common Parent for Code Examples .................. SUCCESS
[0.758s]
[INFO] common ...................................... .... .... ..
SUCCESS [0.634s]
[INFO] Code samples for Chapter 2 ....................... SUCCESS
[0.045s]
[INFO] Code samples for Chapter 3 ....................... SUCCESS
[0.030s]
[INFO] Code samples for Chapter 4 ....................... SUCCESS
[0.027s]
[INFO] Code samples for Chapter 6 ....................... SUCCESS
[0.025s]
[INFO] Code samples for Chapter 7 ....................... SUCCESS
[0.042s]
[INFO] ------------------------------------------------------------------
```

```
------
[INFO] BUILD SUCCESS
[INFO] ------------------------------------------------------------------
------
```

Next, we will pack our project so that we generate the `common-1.0.0-SNAPSHOT.jar` file containing the common input-output libraries used by the examples:

```
C:\infinispan-Infinispan-book>mvn install
[INFO] ------------------------------------------------------------------
------
[INFO] BUILD SUCCESS
[INFO] ------------------------------------------------------------------
------
[INFO] Total time: 4.882s
[INFO] Finished at: Tue Jun 19 22:07:34 CEST 2012
[INFO] Final Memory: 5M/15M
[INFO] ------------------------------------------------------------------
------
```

If you have followed the instructions so far, you will end up with a fully compiled project. There are several viable options to run your project's main classes; the simplest one may be executing the `mvn exec:java` command, which requires the main class as argument to launch:

```
C:\infinispan-Infinispan-book>cd chapter2
C:\infinispan-Infinispan-book\chapter2>mvn exec:java -Dexec.
mainClass="com.packtpub.infinispan.chapter2.SimpleCache"
```

The preceding command will execute the first example that we have introduced in this chapter.

Summary

In this chapter, we have discussed the Infinispan Cache API, which exposes, at its core, a Cache interface that extends `java.util.Map`, overriding the base methods used to add, remove, or get data from the cache. Infinispan has some unique features that do not exist in the `java.util` API, such as setting data expiration for the entries, implementing listeners, and participating in JTA transactions.

Up to now, the examples have been based on the default Infinispan configuration. In the next chapter, we will dissect the core Infinispan configuration file and will also learn how to use a programmatic configuration API to achieve the same results.

3

Introducing Infinispan Configuration

Infinispan is designed to operate in many different environments and, as such, there is a broad range of configuration parameters. Fortunately, most have sensible default values, and so you can even run your applications using zero configuration, as we did in the previous chapter.

However, when you are using non-default configurations (such as a clustered one), you need to learn the basics of the configuration. You can use two approaches to configure Infinispan:

- **Declarative configuration**: This configuration is the most common approach, as it relies on an XML file, which is parsed when Infinispan starts
- **Programmatic configuration**: This kind of configuration is done through the Infinispan API and it is, therefore, a useful approach if your application needs to dynamically configure Infinispan

In this chapter, we will demonstrate both approaches, with a focus on the basic configuration elements, while in the next chapter, we will discuss advanced topics, such as clustering and transactions.

Learning the declarative configuration

Handling the configuration in an XML file is the most popular choice among developers. This choice helps to keep your project tidy, as you have your entire configuration in one place. Additionally, the configuration can be changed at deployment time, thus not requiring recompilation of your classes.

The main difference from an application that does not use a configuration file is in the constructor of the `CacheManager` object, which optionally takes in a URL to a configuration XML file, as shown here:

```
CacheManager manager = new DefaultCacheManager("config-file.xml");
```

The XML configuration that is used by Infinispan contains the Infinispan root node, beneath which you have the following set of elements (all of which are optional):

- `global`: This element defines the global settings shared among all cache instances created by a single cache manager. The following diagram shows the XML elements that can be included in the `global` section:

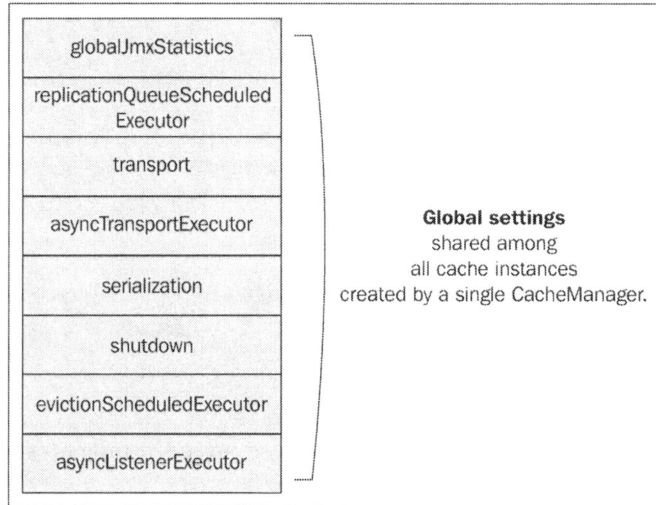

- `default`: This element specifies the default behavior for all the named caches belonging to this cache manager.
- `namedCache`: This element specifies additional configuration elements for specific named caches, and will extend what is defined in `default`.

Both the `default` section and the `namedCache` section can contain the same list of elements, as shown in the following diagram:

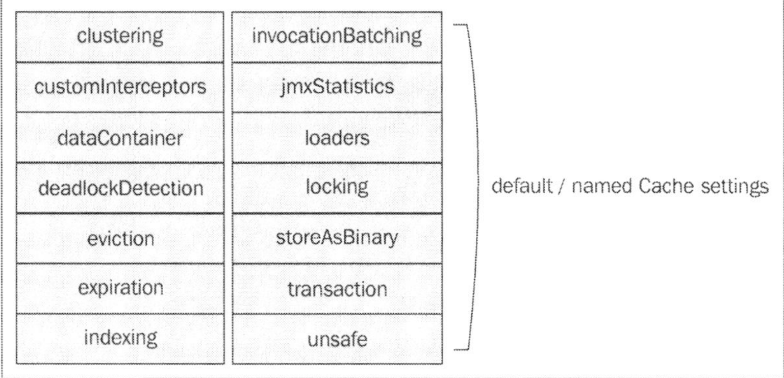

In the next section, we will briefly discuss the global settings, just after we cover the cache settings that can be applied to every named cache (`default`) or to a specific cache (`namedCache`), in greater detail.

Global configuration settings

The global configuration section contains mostly some low-level settings, which should be of interest for experienced users. Most of these settings are related to controlling thread pools, serialization, or with configuring a network data transport.

The following table reviews them with a short description for each:

Element	**Description**
`asyncListenerExecutor`	Configures the executor service used to emit notifications to asynchronous listeners.
`asyncTransportExecutor`	Configuration for the executor service used for asynchronous work on the transport, including asynchronous marshalling and cache async operations such as `Cache.putAsync()`.
`evictionScheduledExecutor`	Configuration for the scheduled executor service used to periodically run eviction cleanup tasks.
`replicationQueueScheduledExecutor`	Configuration for the scheduled executor service used to periodically flush replication queues; used if asynchronous clustering is enabled along with `useReplQueue` being set to `true`.

Element	Description
`globalJmxStatistics`	This element specifies whether global statistics are gathered and reported via JMX for all caches under this cache manager.
`transport`	This element configures the transport used for network communications across the cluster.
`serialization`	Configures serialization and marshalling settings.
`shutdown`	This element specifies behavior when the JVM running the cache instance shuts down.

And here's a sample global configuration section, which contains some of the aforementioned elements:

```
<global>

    <asyncListenerExecutor factory=
      "org.infinispan.executors.DefaultExecutorFactory">
        <properties>
          <property name="maxThreads" value="5"/>
          <property name="threadNamePrefix"
            value="AsyncListenerThread"/>
        </properties>
    </asyncListenerExecutor>

    <asyncTransportExecutor factory=
      "org.infinispan.executors.DefaultExecutorFactory">
        <properties>
          <property name="maxThreads" value="25"/>
          <property name="threadNamePrefix"
            value="AsyncSerializationThread"/>
        </properties>
    </asyncTransportExecutor>

    <evictionScheduledExecutor factory=
      "org.infinispan.executors.DefaultScheduledExecutorFactory">
        <properties>
          <property name="threadNamePrefix"
            value="EvictionThread"/>
        </properties>
    </evictionScheduledExecutor>
```

```
    <globalJmxStatistics enabled="true"
            jmxDomain="org.infinispan"
            cacheManagerName="SampleCacheManager"/>

    <transport
        clusterName = "MyCluster"
        machineId = "LinuxServer01"
        rackId = "Rack01"
        siteId = "Western-Europe" />
    </transport>

</global>
```

The first Executor, `asyncListenerExecutor`, defines a maximum of five threads that are used as asynchronous listeners. We remind you that the Infinispan listeners, by default, are synchronous, but you can alter this behavior by setting the `sync = false` parameter to the `@Listener` annotation (see *Chapter 2, Using Infinispan Core API*, for more information about listeners), as shown here:

```
@Listener (sync = false)
public class MyAsyncListener { .... }
```

Next, `asyncTransportExecutor` comes into play, if you intend to use the non-blocking, asynchronous API, or if you have configured your cluster to use asynchronous communications (see the next chapter for more information about clustering configuration).

Then, `evictionScheduledExecutor` can be used, if you have eviction enabled and wish to customize the executor used by the eviction and expiration process.

The `globalJmxStatistics` element enables the collection of global JMX statistics and allows you to customize the JMX domain name, under which MBeans are registered (see *Chapter 5, Monitoring Infinispan*, for more information about monitoring Infinispan).

Finally, the `transport` element configures the transport used for network communications across the cluster. The first parameter, `clusterName`, defines the name of the cluster. When specified, your cluster nodes will only connect to clusters sharing the same name. The other settings can be used to ensure that, when using data distribution, the backups are not picked to reside on a node on the same physical server, rack, or data center. This is also known as **server hinting**.
Let's look at the settings in a bit more detail:

- `machineId`: This can be useful to disambiguate between multiple JVM instances on the same node, or even multiple virtual hosts on the same physical host

- `rackId`: In larger clusters, with nodes occupying more than a single rack, this setting would help prevent backups being stored on the same rack, to guard against the failure of an entire rack
- `siteId`: For very large networks, `siteId` can be used to differentiate between nodes in different data centers, replicating to each other

We will provide more details about clustering and network transport in the next chapter, which covers advanced Infinispan configuration.

Cache configuration settings

Both the `default` and `namedCache` sections share the same set of elements that will be either used for all caches (`default`) or for a specific cache (`namedCache`). For example, in the following configuration snippet, we are defining the data eviction for all caches in the same cache manager:

```
<infinispan>
  <default>
    <eviction strategy="LRU" maxEntries="2000"/>
  </default>
</infinispan>
```

Here's how you can then customize it for a specific named cache:

```
<infinispan>
  <namedCache name="evictionCache">
    <eviction strategy="LIRS" maxEntries="2000"/>
  </namedCache>
</infinispan>
```

The main difference is that you can reference the default cache using the well-known `getCache` method:

```
Cache defaultCache = manager.getCache();
```

On the other hand, a specific cache can be retrieved by passing the cache name to the `getCache` method:

```
Cache someNamedCache = manager.getCache("someNamedCache");
```

The list of elements that can be included in the default/named cache covers all the details of the cache configuration. The following table describes them synthetically:

Configuration element	Description
`clustering`	Defines clustered characteristics of the cache.
`customInterceptors`	Configures custom interceptors to be added to the cache.
`dataContainer`	Controls the data container for the cache.
`deadlockDetection`	Configures deadlock detection.
`eviction`	Controls the eviction settings for the cache.
`expiration`	Controls the default expiration settings for entries in the cache.
`indexing`	Configures indexing of entries in the cache for searching.
`invocationBatching`	Defines whether invocation batching is allowed in this cache instance and sets up internals accordingly, to allow use of this API.
`jmxStatistics`	Determines whether statistics are gathered and reported.
`loaders`	Configuration for cache loaders and stores.
`locking`	Defines the local, in-VM locking and concurrency characteristics of the cache.
`storeAsBinary`	Controls whether when stored in memory, keys and values are stored as references to their original objects, or in a serialized, binary format.
`transaction`	Defines transactional (JTA) characteristics of the cache.
`unsafe`	Controls certain tuning parameters that may break some of Infinispan's public API contracts in exchange for better performance in some cases.

As you can see, the number of configuration elements that can be used is quite large. As such, not all elements will be described in detail here; instead, we do the following:

- We will see how to configure cache loaders, data eviction and expiration, and custom interceptors, in the next section.
- We will cover some more advanced topics, such as clustering, transactions, and data locking, in the next chapter.

Configuring cache loaders

A cache loader is the mechanism that reads entries that have been placed in a Cache Store—a form of persistent storage. The entries are fetched from the store lazily, when there is a cache miss (that is, when the entry is not found in memory). When modifications are made to the data in memory, the cache store is notified of the change so that the entry in persistent store can be updated.

> **Some terminology for JBoss Cache users**
>
> JBoss Cache is shipped with a single cache loader interface. Infinispan has broken this up into two separate interfaces—**CacheLoader**, which loads the entries from persistant storage, and **CacheStore**, which extends CacheLoader and exposes methods to store state as well. This makes it simpler to define read-only sources.

You can configure one or more cache loaders using the `loaders` element, as in the following example:

```
<loaders
        passivation="true"
        shared="false"
        preload="false">

        <loader
           class="org.infinispan.loaders.file.FileCacheStore"
           fetchPersistentState="false"
           purgeOnStartup="false">

           <properties>
              <property name="location"
                  value="${java.io.tmpdir}"/>
           </properties>

        </loader>
</loaders>
```

As you can see, the cache loader contains a set of attributes, common to all loaders (included in the top `loaders` element), and the specific cache loader information (included in the children `loader` elements). Let's first look at the common attributes.

Common cache loader attributes

Let us start with the **passivation** attribute. When set to `true`, entries that are evicted are removed from memory, and they are persisted using a cache store (for example, filesystem, database, and others). With passivation enabled (by default it is disabled), the cache uses the cache store just like a swapping memory area in an operating system.

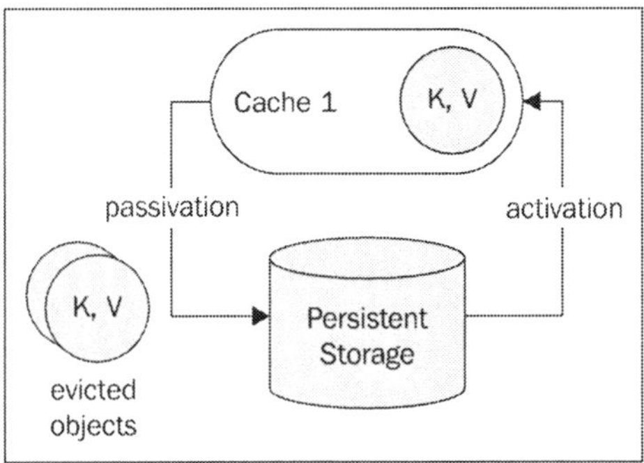

The benefit of this approach is to prevent a lot of expensive writes to the cache store, if an entry is frequently used and hence not evicted from memory. The reverse process, known as **activation**, occurs when a thread attempts to access an entry that is not in the memory but is in the store (that is, a passivated entry). Activation involves loading the entry into memory, and then removing it from the cache store.

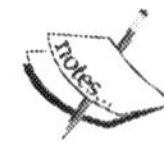

> If passivation is disabled, the cache store behaves as a **write-through cache**, which means that write is done synchronously, both to the cache and to the backing store. On the other hand, a **write-behind cache** is one where data is stored in a backend store using a separate thread, making cache calls return very fast, while at the same time persisting data permanently. These types of caches are particularly interesting for stores with high latency, such as cloud based stores, or remote databases.

The next attribute, `shared`, means that the cache loader is shared among different cache instances in the cluster. This is useful in a clustered environment, in order to prevent repeated and unnecessary writes of the same data to the cache store, by different cache instances (`false` by default).

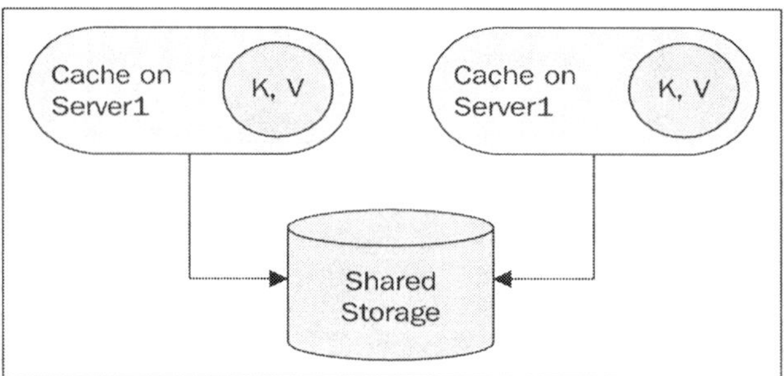

When using a shared cache loader, it means that all nodes have a cache loader that accesses a common shared backend store. This could be, for example, a shared database, so that all nodes access the same store.

Finally, if `preload` is set to `true`, when the cache starts, data stored in the cache loader will be preloaded eagerly into memory. Note that preloading is done per node. No replication or distribution of the preloaded data will happen. Also, Infinispan honors the configured maximum number of entries in eviction, when loading data from the cache; preloading defaults to `false`.

Specific cache loader attributes

Apart from attributes that affect all cache loaders, you can specify some specific attributes for individual cache loaders configured.

The first, most important, and mandatory attribute is `class`. It defines the class of the cache loader implementation. This allows you to pick the actual storage engine to use. Infinispan ships with several implementations, including a a file-based cache store, JDBC-based one, one that persists to cloud storage engines, as well as the ability to write your own implementations.

The `fetchPersistentState` (`false` by default) attribute is used in a clustered environment and determines whether to fetch the persistent state of a cache when joining a cluster and performing a state transfer.

Setting this attribute to `false` will result in a cold cache that gradually warms up as elements are accessed and loaded for the first time. This would mean that individual caches in a cluster might have different in-memory states at any given time (largely depending on their preloading and eviction strategies).

`purgeSynchronously` controls whether the purging of expired items in the cache store takes place in the eviction thread, that is, if `purgeSynchronously` (`false` by default) is set to `true`, the eviction thread will block execution until the purging is finished; otherwise it will return immediately, performing the purging of expired entries in a separate thread.

`ignoreModifications` (`false` by default) determines whether updates are propagated to the cache store. If a store is to be treated as read-only, then `ignoreModifications` should be set to `true`.

`purgeOnStatup` empties the specified cache store (if `ignoreModifications` is `false`), when the cache starts up.

Finally, each cache loader can contain the `properties` element, which holds the configurations specific to each cache loader. For example, the `location` property in the previous example refers to where `FileCacheStore` will maintain files on the local file system to hold data.

Choosing the correct cache store for your application

As we have already learnt, you can opt among several available cache store implementations by setting the appropriate class attribute in your cache loader definition.

In the former example, we have introduced `org.infinispan.loaders.file.FileCacheStore`, which is a filesystem-based implementation. The location on the local file system, where the implementation stores data, is defined as a property, as follows:

```
<loader
   class="org.infinispan.loaders.file.FileCacheStore"
   fetchPersistentState="false"
   purgeOnStartup="false">
   <properties>
      <property name="location" value="${java.io.tmpdir}"/>
   </properties>
</loader>
```

`FileCacheStore` has some limitations, which must be kept in mind:

- Usage on shared filesystems such as NFS, Windows shares, and other similar technologies, should be avoided, as these do not implement proper POSIX file locking, and can cause data corruption
- Filesystems are inherently not transactional, so when attempting to use your cache in a transactional context, failures when writing to the file (which happens during the commit phase) cannot be recovered

As an alternative, you might consider using `org.infinispan.loaders.bdbje.BdbjeCacheStore`, which is a cache store implementation that delegates to Oracle's **BerkeleyDB** Java Edition. The BerkeleyDB implementation is much more efficient than the filesystem-based implementation and provides transactional guarantees, but it requires a commercial license if distributed with an application (see `http://www.oracle.com/database/berkeley-db/index.html` for details).

You might also consider `org.infinispan.loaders.jdbm.JdbmCacheStore`, which is a cache store implementation based on the open-source, B-tree engine known as JDBM.

JDBC-based cache stores

A valid and recommended alternative to filesystem-based cache stores is the JDBC cache store, which persists data in a relational database using a JDBC driver. There are three implementations of the JDBC cache store, which are as follows:

- `JdbcBinaryCacheStore`
- `JdbcStringBasedCacheStore`
- `JdbcMixedCacheStore`

The `JdbcBinaryCacheStore` implementation is a standard JDBC solution that can store any type of key for your entries. This can be achieved by storing all the Map buckets (slot of array elements) as rows into the database. This provides greater flexibility, at the cost of coarse-grained access granularity and inherent performance.

In contrast to `JdbcBinaryCacheStore`, the `JdbcStringBasedCacheStore` implementation will store each entry within a row in the table (rather than grouping multiple entries into a row). This assures a fine-grained granularity for all operations, and better performance than `JdbcBinaryCacheStore`, but it requires that all cache keys are Strings. In order to be able to store non-String keys, it requires that you provide an implementation of the `Key2StringMapper` interface—so that the cache store is able to convert arbitrary key types to Strings, and back again.

Finally, `JdbcMixedCacheStore` is a hybrid implementation that, based on the key type, delegates to either `JdbcBinaryCacheStore` or `JdbcStringBasedCacheStore`, so you have the best of both worlds.

The following is a sample configuration that uses `JdbcStringBasedCacheStore` to store data in a MySQL database:

```
<loaders>
  <loader class=
    "org.infinispan.loaders.jdbc.
    stringbased.JdbcStringBasedCacheStore"
    fetchPersistentState="true"
    ignoreModifications="false"
    purgeOnStartup="false">
    <properties>
      <property name="stringsTableNamePrefix"
        value="ISPN_STRING_TABLE"/>
      <property name="idColumnName"
        value="ID_COLUMN"/>
      <property name="idColumnType"
        value="VARCHAR(255)"/>

      <property name="dataColumnName"
        value="DATA_COLUMN"/>
      <property name="dataColumnType"
        value="TRUE"/>

      <property name="timestampColumnName"
        value="TIMESTAMP_COLUMN"/>
      <property name="timestampColumnType"
        value="BIGINT"/>

      <property name="connectionFactoryClass"
        value="org.infinispan.loaders.jdbc.
        connectionfactory.PooledConnectionFactory"/>
      <property name="connectionUrl"
        value="java:jboss/datasources/MySQLDS"/>
      <property name="userName" value="xxxx"/>
      <property name="password" value="xxxx"/>
      <property name="driverClass"
        value="com.mysql.jdbc.Driver"/>
      <property name="dropTableOnExit"
        value="true"/>
      <property name="createTableOnStart"
        value="true"/>

    </properties>
  </loader>
</loaders>
```

If you have ever configured a JDBC Connection using Hibernate or any other framework that makes use of a JDBC driver, most of these properties should be quite intuitive to you. Basically, `connectionUrl`, `username`, `password`, and `driverClass` define the JDBC Connection settings.

The other settings — `idColumnName`, `idColumnType`, `dataColumnName`, `dataColumnType`, `timestampColumnName`, and `timestampColumnType` — define the structure of the tables used to represent the in-memory data within the database. Furthermore, you can use `createTableOnStart`, which will create the table in the database when the cache starts, and additionally drop the table when you stop the cache, if `dropTableOnExit` is set to `true`.

Chaining cache loaders

At the beginning of this section, we informed you that you could configure one or more cache loaders beneath the loaders element. The effect of defining multiple cache loaders is that they will be chained; this means that, for every **read** operation, they will be searched in the order that they are placed into the XML in, until the data is found. On the other hand, when you are performing a **cache write**, it will span across all the cache stores, unless you set the `ignoreModifications` parameter to `false`, for a specific cache store.

In the following example, we have a chained cache loader configuration, which includes `FileCacheStore` and `CloudCacheStore`:

```
<namedCache name="chainedCacheLoader">
    <loaders passivation="false"
      shared="false" preload="true">
          <loader class=
            "org.infinispan.loaders.file.FileCacheStore"
            fetchPersistentState="false"
            purgeOnStartup="false">
                <properties>
                    <property name="location"
                              value="${java.io.tmpdir}"/>
                </properties>
          </loader>
          <loader class=
            "org.infinispan.loaders.cloud.CloudCacheStore"
            fetchPersistentState="false"
            ignoreModifications="false"
            purgeOnStartup="false">
                <properties>
                    <property name="identity"
```

```
                value="${ec2.access_key}"/>
              <property name="password"
                value="${ec2.access_secret}"/>
              <property name="bucketPrefix"
                value="${ec2.bucket}"/>
              <property name="requestTimeout"
                value="20000"/>
              <property name="cloudService"
                value="s3"/>
              <property name="secure"
                value="true"/>
              <property name="compress"
                value="true"/>
          </properties>
          <async enabled="true"
            flushLockTimeout="15000"
            threadPoolSize="10"
          />
      </loader>
    </loaders>
</namedCache>
```

A Cloud cache loader uses **JClouds** (`http://www.jclouds.org`) to read/write data to a cloud storage provider such as Amazon S3—very useful if your application is deployed in a cloud environment such as Amazon EC2.

A brief note about each of the `CloudCacheStore` properties:

- `identity`: A string that identifies you to the cloud provider. For example, with **Amazon Web Services** (**AWS**), this property is your `ACCESS KEY` element.
- `password`: A string that is used to authenticate you with the cloud provider. For example, with AWS, this is your `SECRET KEY` element.
- `bucketPrefix`: A string that is prepended to generated buckets or containers on the cloud store. Buckets or containers are named `{bucketPrefix}-{cacheName}`.
- `requestTimeout`: A timeout to use when communicating with the cloud storage provider, in milliseconds. Defaults to `10000`.
- `cloudService`: This property indicates the cloud service to use. Supported values are `s3` (Amazon AWS), `cloudfiles` (Rackspace Cloud), `azureblob` (Microsoft Azure), and `atmos` (Atmos Online Storage Service).

- `secure`: This property indicates whether to use secure (SSL) connections; defaults to `true`.
- `compress`: This property indicates whether to compress stored data; defaults to `true`.

Configuring eviction and expiration

Having discussed persistence via cache stores and passivation in detail, we can now look at data expiration and eviction, which are logically related to persisting in-memory data.

Let us consider the following named cache configuration, `evictionCache`, where eviction, expiration as well as a cache store is defined:

```
<infinispan>
 <namedCache name="evictionCache">
    <eviction
        maxEntries="1000"
        strategy="LRU"
     />
     <expiration
        wakeUpInterval="500"
        lifespan="60000"
        maxIdle="10000"
     />
    <loaders passivation="true">
        <loader class="org.infinispan.loaders.file.FileCacheStore">
           <properties>
              <property name="location" value="${java.io.tmpdir}"/>
           </properties>
        </loader>
     </loaders>
 </namedCache>
</infinispan>
```

When using this configuration, no more than 1000 elements will be maintained in memory. If you try to put more entries in your cache, they will be evicted using the **LRU (Least Recently Used)** strategy, which discards the least recently used items first. Since passivation is turned `ON`, the data that is evicted from the cache will be swapped onto disk, via the configured FileCacheStore (with data files located in `java.io.tmpdir`, which is by default `/tmp` on Unix systems, and typically `c:/temp` on Windows machines).

Additionally, it's defined that the expiration thread will run every 500 milliseconds to scan for expired entries. Each entry will, by default, expire in 10,000 milliseconds after it is last accessed, or 60,000 milliseconds after the entry has been created, whichever triggers first.

Testing our ticket system with eviction and passivation

Now we can use the aforementioned configuration to demonstrate eviction and passivation in conjunction with `FileCacheStore`. Save your configuration file in an XML file named `sample.xml` and modify your code accordingly.

We will need to reference our configuration file by name. Also, we have replaced the interactive ticketing system with a random String generator (`UUID.randomUUID().toString()`) so that you can bulk insert 1500 entries (500 of which will be passivated to disk):

```
DefaultCacheManager m
  = new DefaultCacheManager("sample.xml");
        Cache<Integer, Ticket> cache =
          m.getCache("evictionCache");
          int ticketid = 1;

       while (ticketid < 1500){

              String name =
                UUID.randomUUID().toString();
              String show =
                UUID.randomUUID().toString();

              Ticket ticket = new Ticket(name,show);
              cache.put(ticketid, ticket);
              ticketid++;
       }
log("Booked tickets:   "+ticketid);
log("Tickets in memory: "+cache.size());
```

The expected outcome of this example is that, when the amount of entries stored in the cache exceeds the `maxEntries` parameter, the eviction thread will start passivating entries in the location defined in the `FileCacheStore` parameter (in our example `c:\temp`), within the directory named `evictionCache` (the named cache used in this example).

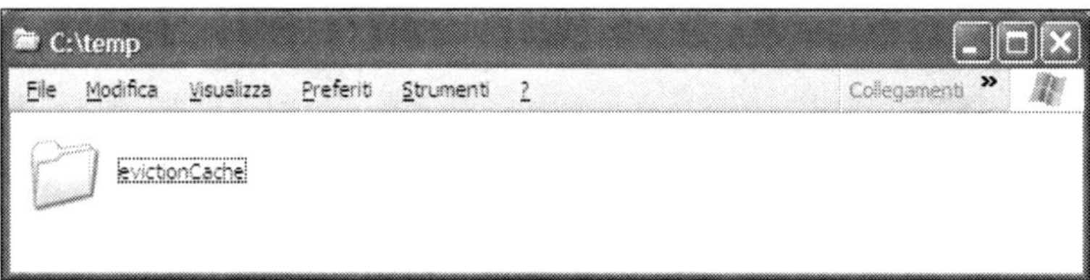

Infinispan programmatic configuration

Programmatic configuration can be used as an alternative to defining your configuration in XML. Everything that has been demonstrated in XML can also be achieved via a powerful, fluent, and easy to use programmatic API. You can also mix and match approaches, by using an XML file to define a base configuration, and then further configuring Infinispan using the programmatic API to override or enhance your static, XML-based configuration. Thus, when setting up the programmatic configuration API, you have two choices:

- Start with a static XML configuration and then modify parts of the configuration before starting the cache
- Start a brand new configuration programmatically, which will be used by your cache

Both of these approaches rely on `org.infinispan.configuration.cache.ConfigurationBuilder` as a factory to create instances of `org.infinispan.configuration.cache.Configuration`, which represents the configuration of a cache. Configuration instances are immutable and cannot be changed once they are created.

The following is an example of reading a configuration from an XML file, using it as a starting point to create new configurations programmatically:

```
DefaultCacheManager manager =
  new DefaultCacheManager("infinispan-config-file.xml");
Configuration baseConf =
  manager.getDefaultCacheConfiguration();
Configuration config =
  new ConfigurationBuilder().
    read(baseConf).
```

```
        expiration().
        lifespan(50000).
        build();
    String programmaticCache = "expiryCache";
    manager.defineConfiguration(programmaticCache, config);
    Cache<String, String> cache =
      manager.getCache(programmaticCache);
```

In this short code snippet, we read a configuration from an XML file — `infinispan-config-file.xml` — which is parsed and used as the default cache, as we have seen before. The contents of the XML file is parsed into a `Configuration` object instance (`config`) and later used as a parameter for the `read` method of `ConfigurationBuilder()`, which initializes the `ConfigurationBuilder`. Once this is done, you use the `ConfigurationBuilder` to further tune your configuration.

In this example, we configure the `expiration` method of entries stored in the cache to have a lifespan of 50,000 milliseconds.

The `build` method on the builder generates a new (and again immutable) Configuration instance, encapsulating your newly customized configuration, which can be passed in the `defineConfiguration` method of the Cache Manager. This will create a new named cache configuration in the Cache Manager and and can be retrieved using `getCache()`.

Creating a configuration from scratch

If you do not wish to start with an XML configuration file, it is just as simple. The previous example can thus be rewritten as:

```
Configuration config =
  new ConfigurationBuilder()
      .expiration().
      .lifespan(50000).
      .build();
```

Let's see an example that is a bit more complex. We will suppose that you need to programmatically add a `FileCacheStore`, which uses `C:\\temp` as its storage location and sets the properties `passivation`, `shared`, and `preload`:

```
Configuration config =
    new ConfigurationBuilder()
      .loaders()
      .shared(false)
      .passivation(true)
```

```
            .preload(false)
            .addFileCacheStore()
            .location("C:\\temp")
            .build();
```

As you may have noticed, the `ConfigurationBuilder` API contains equivalent methods for every XML element you may have seen in the XML configuration file (in this case the `loaders` method). This helps make the configuration more readable and familiar.

`ConfigurationBuilder` also supports the generic `addCacheLoader` method, which can be used to define cache loaders based on a fully qualified class name; for example, here's how we could add the `JdbcStringBasedCacheStore` implementation, which we have introduced in the *JDBC-based cache stores* section of this chapter.
This technique will also work for a custom-built cache store:

```
Configuration config =
  new ConfigurationBuilder()
  .loaders()
    .shared(false).passivation(false).preload(false)
.addCacheLoader()
    .cacheLoader(new JdbcStringBasedCacheStore())
    .addProperty("connectionFactoryClass",
      "org.infinispan.loaders.jdbc
      .connectionfactory.ManagedConnectionFactory")
    .addProperty("datasourceJndiLocation", "java:jboss/datasources/
MySQLDS")
    .addProperty("idColumnType", "VARCHAR(255)")
    .addProperty("idColumnName", "ID_COLUMN")
    .addProperty("dataColumnType", "BINARY")
    .addProperty("dataColumnName", "DATA_COLUMN")
    .addProperty("timestampColumnName", "TIMESTAMP_COLUMN")
    .addProperty("timestampColumnType", "BIGINT")
    .addProperty("stringsTableNamePrefix", "ISPN_STRING_TABLE")
    .addProperty("userName", "root")
    .addProperty("password", "admin")
    .async().threadPoolSize(10)
    .build();
```

Creating the Global configuration programmatically

Programmatic configuration is not limited to what you see in the `default` (and `named` cache) sections in the XML file. You can also use it for configuring global settings, just as we demonstrated in the *Global configuration settings* section.

Instead of using the `Configuration` object, we will use the `org.infinispan.configuration.global.GlobalConfiguration` class, which represents global settings. Supposing you need to set the number of threads used by `asyncListenerExecutor`; you would do the following:

```
GlobalConfiguration gc = new GlobalConfigurationBuilder()
     .asyncListenerExecutor()
     .addProperty("maxThreads", "200").build();
```

Summary

In this chapter, we have covered some common configuration options that are available in Infinispan.

We explored both declarative and programmatic configuration (and even a mix of them) to determine how Infinispan behaves.

Each configuration is composed of three main elements:

- `global`: This section affects all cache instances created by a single cache manager.
- `default`: This section defines the behavior of a specific cache, and is used to configure the default cache obtained using `CacheManager.getCache()`.
- `namedCache`: This section defines the configuration for specific named caches. Named caches inherit the configuration of the default cache first, which is then overridden by any configuration defined in a `namedCache` section.

Next, we covered the configuration of cache loaders, which is used for storing in-memory data onto a more persistent storage mechanism.

Then we discussed the configuration of data eviction and expiration, with an example that involves passivation of data to a persistent store.

In the next chapter, we are going to discuss more advanced topics, such as clustering and transaction configuration.

4

Developing Advanced Configurations

This chapter introduces some advanced topics, such as clustering and transactions, that are essential for scalable and reliable Enterprise applications. We will cover the following topics:

- Configuring the network transport
- Creating an Infinispan cluster
- Locking and transactions in Infinispan

Introducing clustering

In order to get started with clustering, it is essential that some basic concepts are clear to the reader. A cluster consists of a number of Infinispan instances, known as **members** of a cluster. Each member has an **address** that uniquely identifies this member. An address maps to a **physical** address (such as an IP address and port) but may have a logical name. Each cluster in turn has a **view**, which is the list of cluster members at any given point in time. The view is always consistent (that is, the same for all members) and will be updated when members join or leave a cluster.

Members communicate with one another by sending messages around a cluster. Messages contain the contents of a given communication, as well as the sender's and receiver's address. Members can only send or receive messages after they've joined a cluster.

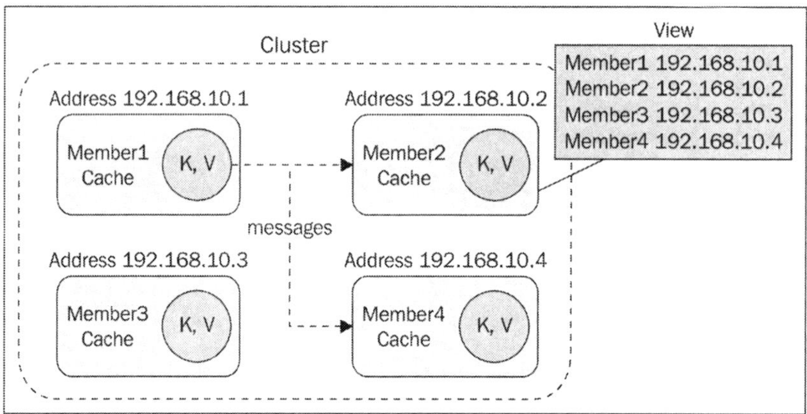

This diagram depicts a cluster of members; however, what happens when a new member joins the cluster? That instance has to somehow get some (or all) of the collective data held in the cluster to be useful. This process is called **state transfer**, and it's essential to provide one of the key benefits of clustered applications—high availability.

In order to get started with clustering, we will at first detail how messages are moved across the cluster.

Configuring the network transport

Infinispan makes use of **JGroups**—an open source reliable messaging toolkit—for communications within a cluster as well as discovery of new or failed members.

By default, you don't need to provide a JGroups configuration file, as defaults are provided in the `infinispan-core.jar` file. Therefore, you can choose among the following built-in configuration files:

- `jgroups-udp.xml`: It uses UDP as transport and UDP multicast for discovery. The file is usually suitable for larger (over 100 nodes) clusters or if you are using replication or invalidation. This choice minimizes opening too many sockets.

- `jgroups-tcp.xml`: This file uses TCP as transport and UDP multicast for discovery. This solution works better for smaller clusters (under 100 nodes), and even better if you are using data distribution, considering that TCP is more efficient as a point-to-point protocol. Discovery is still performed using UDP multicast.
- `jgroups-ec2.xml`: This option uses TCP as transport protocol and the experimental S3_PING protocol for discovery. It is suitable on those Amazon EC2 nodes where UDP multicast isn't available.

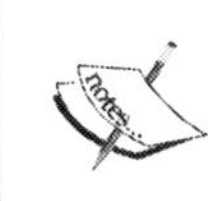

The choice of the network transport depends on many things, including the characteristics of your network, the size and type of your data, and the characteristics of your data access patterns; but it also depends on your replication model. See the *Choosing between replication and distribution* section for more information.

By default, Infinispan will use the file called `jgroups-udp.xml`, which is shipped with Infinispan. Here is an example of how to point to the `jgroups-tcp.xml` file shipped with Infinispan as your transport:

```
<infinispan>
  <global>
    <transport>
      <properties>
        <property name="configurationFile" value="jgroups-tcp.xml" />
      </properties>
    </transport>
  </global>
   ...
</infinispan>
```

If you want to fine-tune your JGroups stack to extract every ounce of performance from your network, you can also provide your own custom JGroups configuration file and point to it instead. As a starting point to building your own custom JGroups configuration, some samples are available in the `etc/config-samples` directory of the Infinispan distribution. Configuring the underlying transport, however, requires a sound knowledge of JGroups, and is out of the scope of this book. We recommend, as further reading, the JGroups documentation, which has a detailed section on configuring each of the protocols you see in a JGroups configuration file (`http://www.jgroups.org/manual/html/index.html`).

The JGroups configuration also provides a simple, command-line way to customize some common attributes related to the network transport, such as IP addresses and ports to use; it just requires passing some arguments to the JVM at startup.

For example:

```
java -cp ... -Djgroups.udp.mcast_addr=228.10.10.10 -Djgroups.udp.mcast_
port=45588 -Djgroups.udp.ip_ttl =5
```

With the aforementioned settings, we are setting the multicast address (`jgroups.udp.mcast_addr`), port (`jgroups.udp.mcast_port`), and time to live (`jgroups.udp.ip_ttl`) for UDP communications.

> If you are using Infinispan in client/server mode, a good place to add these properties is the `startServer.sh/startServer.cmd` file. If you are using it embedded within a JVM, such as the application server, just inject these flags into the application server startup script.

On the other hand, if you are using TCP as transport, you could, for example, set the TCP port (`jgroups.tcp.port`) and address (`jgroups.tcp.address`), which are used for communication:

```
java ... -Djgroups.tcp.port=1999 -Djgroups.tcp.address=192.168.10.1
```

Again, for a comprehensive list of supported command-line properties, refer to the JGroups documentation.

Creating the Infinispan cluster

The Infinispan can be configured to run in local mode or in a cluster.

> **Why use Infinispan in local mode?**
>
> Although Infinispan delivers its best potential as a distributed data grid, it is still extremely useful as a local data cache.
>
> As we have learned, Infinispan offers features such as eviction and expiration, persistence, JTA and XA compatible transactions, as well as monitoring via JMX, all wrapped around a highly concurrent data container that is heavily tuned for modern multi-core CPUs.

Configuring Infinispan for clustering is , at its most basic, just a case of defining a transport in your global configuration:

```
<global>
    <transport
          nodeName="Infinispan-Node1"
          clusterName="infinispan-cluster" >
```

```
    </transport>
</global>
```

The most important setting is `clusterName`, which defines the name of the cluster. Members only connect to other members sharing the same cluster name. Additionally, you can configure `nodeName`, which is a more user-friendly name of the current member, and will appear in your logs and in JMX. If not specified, the node name defaults to a combination of the host name and a random number (to differentiate multiple nodes on the same host). This transport is shared by all clustered caches owned by a given Cache Manager instance.

The second part of a clustered configuration is in the `clustering` element of the default (or namedCache) section of your configuration file.

Consider the following namedcache configuration:

```
<namedCache name="clusteredCache">
    <clustering mode="replication">
        <stateTransfer
            chunkSize="0"
            fetchInMemoryState = "false"
            timeout ="240000">
        </stateTransfer>

        <sync replTimeout="20000"/>
    </clustering>
</namedCache>
```

The first parameter (`mode`) determines the clustering cache mode. You can choose from **replication**, **distribution**, and **invalidation**.

When using replication, data stored on each node is replicated to all the other nodes of the cluster. This provides very high availability as well as very efficient scalability when reading data (data is always local on every member!), but unfortunately, it does not scale well for writes.

For this reason, the default clustering mode is distribution, which uses more sophisticated techniques (such as consistent hashing to determine data owners, and local caching of remote lookups) to provide linear scalability for writes and predictable and stable performance for reads.

Finally, invalidation is a clustered mode that does not actually share any data at all but simply aims to remove data that may be stale from remote caches. The effect of this is that your cluster will consist of several standalone, "local mode" caches that are network-aware, and will be able to invalidate stale data even if the modifications that make data stale occur remotely. The benefit of this is two-fold:

- The network traffic is minimized as the invalidation messages are very small compared to actually replicating updated data.
- The other caches in the cluster look up modified data in a lazy manner, only when needed. Invalidation is the recommended clustering mode when Infinispan is used as a second level cache for Hibernate. For example, where an external source of data in the event of a cache miss is available.

Next, the `stateTransfer` attribute configures how a state is retrieved when a new member joins the cluster.

You can use the following set of attributes to configure the characteristics of `stateTransfer`:

Attribute	Description
`chunkSize`	If this parameter is greater than zero the state will be transferred in batches of cache entries. Otherwise, the state will be transferred in, all at once. We do not advise changing this setting .
`fetchInMemoryState`	If `true`, this attribute will cause the cache to ask neighboring caches for their state when it starts up, so the cache starts warm, although it will impact startup time.
`timeout`	This is the maximum amount of time—in milliseconds—to wait for the state from neighboring caches, before throwing an exception and aborting startup.

As you can see in the previous example, we have configured our cluster to not to use state transfer (`fetchInMemoryState = false`), which means that when a new member joins a cluster, no data will be fetched at startup.

Another parameter that we have added to our configuration is `sync`, which means that all communications are `synchronous`—whenever your application stores data in Inifnispan, the application thread will block until the appropriate message is sent to the rest of the cluster, and acknowledgements are received. This element is mutually exclusive with the `async` element, which is used to configure an offline, "fire and forget" style of network communications.

Configuring our application to use clustering

Now that we have learned the basics of cluster configuration, we will test our Ticket Booking example in a cluster. For this purpose, save the configuration file (which we introduced at the beginning of this section) as `cluster.xml` and add it to our Ticket Booking system.

As far as the code is concerned, the only change that is needed is to retrieve the appropriate named cache, as follows:

```
DefaultCacheManager m =
    new DefaultCacheManager("cluster.xml");

Cache<Integer, Ticket>
    cache = m.getCache("clusteredCache");
```

Now, start as many instances of your Ticket Booking example as you like (within the limits of your operating system's hardware!) and add some entries to your caches:

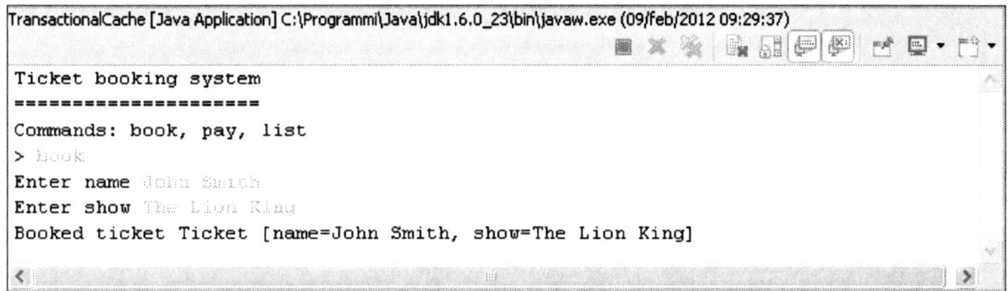

Now switch to another JVM console and verify that data has been replicated to the other nodes of the cache:

```
TransactionalCache [Java Application] C:\Programmi\Java\jdk1.6.0_23\bin\javaw.exe (09/feb/2012 09:29:37)
Ticket booking system
=====================
Commands: book, pay, list
> list
Ticket [name=John Smith, show=The Lion King]
>
```

Accordingly, when you remove an entry from the cache, it will be removed from the other cluster instances as well.

As a final note, bear in mind that in this example we are using a replicated cache with `fetchInMemoryState = false`. This means that the nodes that will subsequently join the cluster will not attempt to fetch state from other members in the cluster. Setting `fetchInMemoryState` to `true`, which will allow for a prepopulated cache from the start, although this will impact the startup time.

Choosing between replication and distribution

Having wet our feet with a simple example, we will now go into more detail on clustering. Specifically, how to choose between replication and distribution clustering modes.

All clustering modes provide for automatic discovery of new members in a cluster, as well as failed members. What happens next depends on the specific clustering mode in question.

Replication is the simplest clustered mode. After a new member joins a cluster, if state transfer is enabled, the new member will receive a copy of the data stored elsewhere in the cluster, so it starts fully populated. After this point, the new member is ready to participate in the cluster.

Each time your application stores data on any member in the cluster, the update will be replicated to all other members in the cluster. Thus, data can be read from any of these cluster members efficiently, as it would be stored locally. This provides for a very high degree of read-scalability, and is extremely useful for read-heavy applications with relatively small data sets. Furthermore, replication provides for a quick and easy way to share state across a cluster.

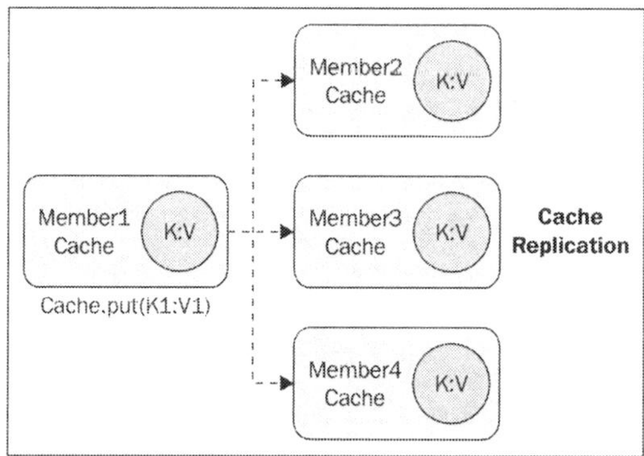

Replication, however, comes at a cost: additional network communications for each and every update. And this cost increases with the size of your cluster. You can mitigate this problem by configuring Infinispan to use UDP multicast, which is capable of broadcasting a single update to all cluster members.

Replication can be **synchronous** or **asynchronous**. Asynchronous replication is faster (no caller blocking), because synchronous replication requires acknowledgments from all nodes in a cluster (that they received and applied successfully, increasing the round-trip time). However, when a synchronous update returns successfully, the caller has a guarantee that the update has been successfully applied to all members in the cluster, whereas this is not the case with asynchronous replication.

Asynchronous replication can take advantage of a replication queue, where updates are batched together and replicated periodically (based on a time interval) or when the queue size exceeds a number of elements or a combination thereof. A replication queue can therefore offer much higher performance, as a background thread performs the actual replication, and the cost of the replication is shared over multiple updates.

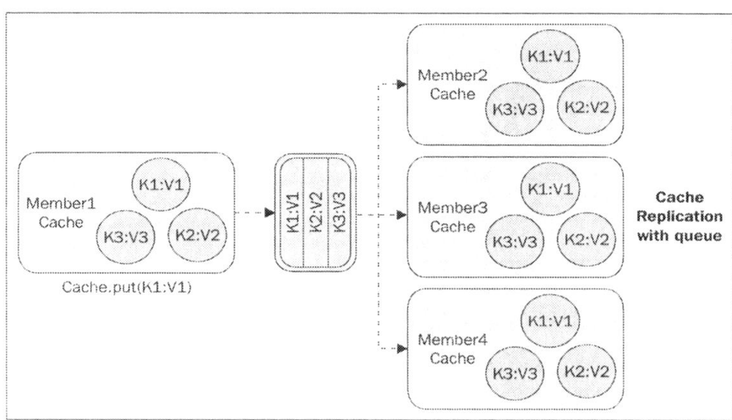

The following example shows how to configure a cluster for asynchronous replication, using a replication queue:

```
<clustering mode="replication">

        <stateRetrieval
           timeout="240000"
           fetchInMemoryState="false"
           alwaysProvideInMemoryState="false"
        />
         <async
           useReplQueue="true"
           replQueueInterval="10000"
```

```
            replQueueMaxElements="500"
        />

</clustering>
```

In this example, setting `useReplQueue` to `true` forces all asynchronous communications to be queued up and sent out periodically, as a batch. `replQueueInterval` controls how often the asynchronous thread should flush the replication queue. This should be a positive integer that represents the thread wakeup time in milliseconds. Finally, `replQueueMaxElements` can be used to trigger flushing of the queue when it reaches a specific threshold.

The other clustering mode is **distribution**, which is the default clustering mode for Infinispan, because it allows for linear write-scalability regardless of cluster size. Distribution makes use of a **consistent hash algorithm** to determine where in a cluster the entries should be stored and how many copies of each piece of data should be maintained cluster-wide.

> Consistent hashing is a well-understood technique for storing data in distributed storage systems. For more information on this algorithm, please refer to `http://weblogs.java.net/blog/tomwhite/archive/2007/11/consistent_hash.html`.

The following is a sample distribution configuration:

```
<clustering mode="distribution">
        <sync/>
        <hash
            numOwners="3"
            rehashEnabled="true"
            rehashRpcTimeout="600000"
        />
</clustering>
```

This configuration uses synchronous calls to dispatch information on the wire. The most interesting section is contained in the **hash** element, where you can configure the number of cluster-wide replicas through the `numOwners` parameter.

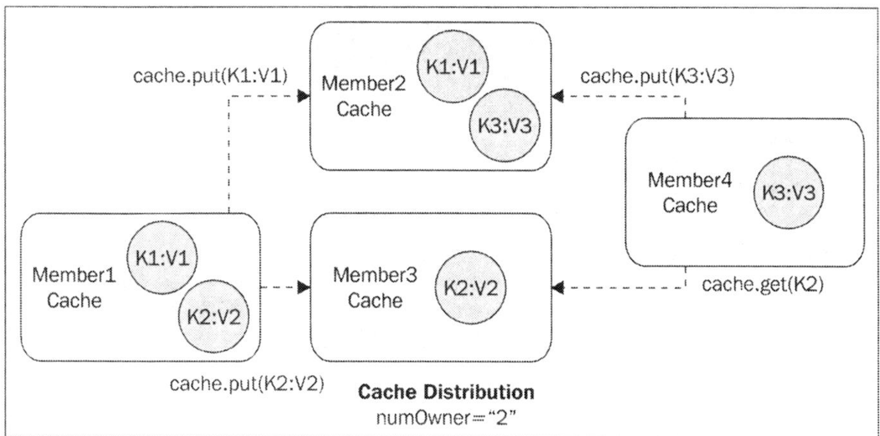

There is an obvious trade-off between the performance and availability of data, as the more copies of data you maintain, the lower performance will be. On the other hand, fewer copies of your data will expose you to the risk of losing data due to server outages.

Additionally, `rehashEnabled`, when set to `true`, causes the rehashing of entries to take place, when a new node joins the cluster or a node leaves, within the timeout expressed by `rehashRpcTimeout`. Rehashing is, effectively, state transfer, except that instead of receiving all cluster-wide state, a new member will only receive a select sub-set of state.

Advanced data distribution

Distribution is a powerful clustering mode that can further be enhanced with some advanced settings. We will first show how to prevent uneven distribution of data throughout the cluster, using virtual nodes. Next, we will detail how to improve the performance of data retrieval, using a mechanism called the **L1 cache**.

Improving the distribution of data with virtual nodes

Infinispan uses a consistent hash algorithm to locate an entry in a cluster. This technique is deterministic, fast, and does not rely on any additional metadata or cluster-wide broadcasts to locate data. This reduces the cost of performing reads and writes on any given member in the cluster, but more importantly, it improves redundancy, as there is no need to replicate the ownership information in case of node failure.

Although using a consistent hash function has positive effects on network traffic, it can lead to poor distribution of data in the cluster, as it relies on the hash code of an entry's key. Poor hashcode implementations and inevitable collisions contribute to such inequal distribution.

In order to mitigate this problem, Infinispan uses a concept called **virtual nodes**. The concept simply allocates multiple slices of the hash wheel to each member in the cluster, and not just one.

Assume a cluster of 3 members, A, B, and C. In the left circle, in the following diagram, we are representing the whole hash space without the virtual nodes. As you can see, node C has a far greater portion of the overall dataset than A or B:

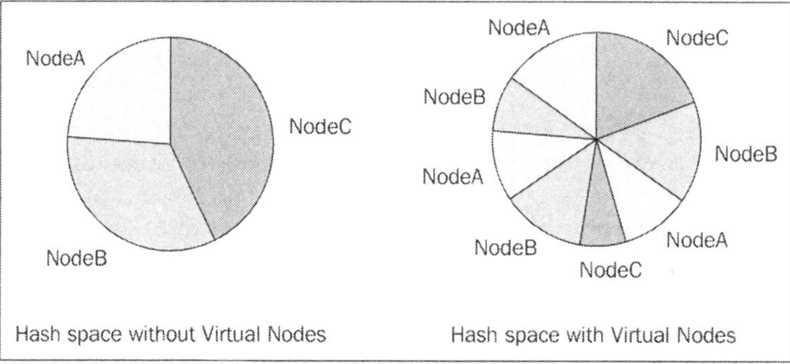

When turning on virtual nodes (the right circle), each member is allocated multiple segments of the hash wheel, thereby reducing the standard deviation and improving the distribution of data. The configuration is done via the `numVirtualNodes` attribute in the `hash` element:

```
<clustering mode="distribution">
         <sync/>
         <hash numOwners="2"
          numVirtualNodes="50"
         />
         />
</clustering>
```

The parameter `numVirtualNodes` controls the number of virtual nodes per real node. If `numVirtualNodes` is `1`, virtual nodes are disabled. In the next chapter, which is about monitoring Infinispan, we will show how to monitor the distribution of data in a cluster.

Using the L1 cache to prevent unnecessary remote calls

An L1 cache can be used to prevent unnecessary lookups of entries that are not locally available to a given member in the cluster. L1 caching essentially caches such entries locally for a short time, after the first time they are retrieved from a remote source. By default, entries in L1 cache have a lifespan of 60,000 milliseconds.
Here is a sample configuration that uses the default values for the L1 cache:

```
<clustering mode="distribution">
        <sync/>
        <l1
            enabled="true"
            lifespan="60000"
        />
</clustering>
```

As you can see from the following image, if L1 is enabled, a subsequent `get` method for the same key on **Server1** would not result in any remote calls:

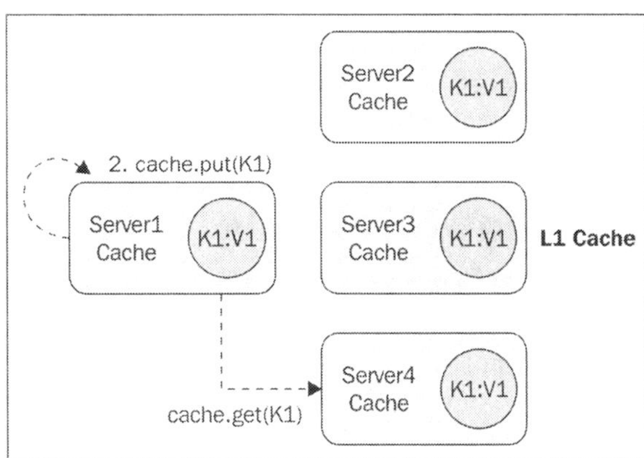

L1 caching is not free, though. Enabling it comes at a cost—every time a key is updated, an invalidation message needs to be multicast to ensure nodes with the entry in L1 invalidate the entry. Furthermore, this adds a memory overhead as L1 caches take up space. So, in order to understand whether L1 caching is worth using in your application, you should benchmark your application with and without L1-enabled caches, and see what works best for your access pattern.

Infinispan locking strategies

Whenever you plan to replicate or distribute your data across several cluster nodes, you must be aware that your data can be accessed or modified concurrently, by several threads. In order to handle concurrent access, Infinispan makes use of some key features of **Multi-Versioned Concurrency Control** (**MVCC**), a technique commonly adopted by relational databases and other data stores.

Infinispan does not explicitly implement MVCC, but just some key features of it.

These features ensure high-level performance, especially for applications that mostly read data, where:

- Concurrent readers and writers are allowed
- Readers and writers do not block one another
- Write skews can be detected and handled
- Internal locks can be striped

Such locking is an integral part of Infinispan's consistency model, however some aspects of this is configurable and can be tuned.

Configuring isolation levels

Most relational databases offer a number of transaction isolation levels that control the degree of isolation that occurs between concurrent threads reading or writing to the same item of data. Infinispan offers two isolation levels: **READ_COMMITTED** (the default) and **REPEATABLE_READ**, which are configurable via the `locking` XML element.

The following table shows the differences between these two isolation levels:

Isolation level	Description
`READ_COMMITTED`	In this isolation level, a thread sees changes performed by a concurrent thread as soon as the concurrent thread commits its transaction. As such, it may see multiple different values for a given entry, based on who else is concurrently modifying that entry.
`REPEATABLE_READ`	In this isolation level, a thread sees a consistent snapshot of any given entry, even if concurrent threads update the entry. As such, it may see historic values of an entry, but this will be stable and consistent with a previous lookup in the same transaction.

The default isolation level used by Infinispan is `READ_COMMITTED`, which also performs the best, and is generally good enough for most applications. If you think you need a higher isolation level, you can opt for `REPEATABLE_READ`, which allows for an additional safety check known as `writeSkewCheck`:

```
<locking
   isolationLevel="REPEATABLE_READ"
   writeSkewCheck="false"
   concurrencyLevel="5000"
/>
```

When `writeSkewCheck` is set to `false` (the default), if an entry has changed between the time it was read and the time it was committed, the latest update will overwrite the underlying entry (last commit wins). If it is set to `true`, and a version conflict exists (known as a write-skew), it will throw an exception and prevent the transaction from completing.

Warning

`writeSkewCheck` only applies if you are using **optimistic** locking. If are configured to use **pessimistic** locking, `writeSkewCheck` will be ignored. See the next section for more information about optimistic and pessimistic locking and transactions.

The other parameter that is included in this example is `concurrencyLevel`. This parameter (actually an integer that defaults to 32) suggests the concurrency level for lock containers. Adjust this value according to the number of concurrent threads you expect to interact with Infinispan. Ideally, you should choose a value to accommodate as many threads, as it will ever concurrently modify data in Infinispan. Using a significantly higher value than you need can waste space and time, and a significantly lower value can lead to thread contention and poor concurrency.

Data locking and transactions

As we have introduced in *Chapter 2, Learning Infinispan Core API*, Infinispan is able to participate in a JTA transaction, just like you would do for a database connection or a JMS message. By default, the operations performed on an Infinispan cache are not running in a transaction; this behavior is pretty much like a JDBC Connection that has `autoCommit` set to `true`.

Transactions are configured on a per-cache basis, using the `transaction` element, as shown in the following example:

```
<namedCache name="transactional">

  <transaction
      transactionManagerLookupClass="org.infinispan.transaction.
      lookup.GenericTransactionManagerLookup"
      transactionMode="TRANSACTIONAL"
      lockingMode="OPTIMISTIC"/>

</namedCache>
```

In order to allow Infinispan to talk to your JTA transaction manager, you need a **transaction manager lookup class**. Infinispan, by default, ships with several transaction manager lookup classes; each one with the ability to locate and detect different JTA transaction managers. The following table describes the transaction manager lookup classes that ship with Infinispan:

Transaction LookupClass	Description
`GenericTransactionManagerLookup`	This lookup class can be used if you are using Infinispan within a Java EE-compatible environment that provides a `TransactionManager` interface, and works with most popular Java EE application servers.
`JBossTransactionManagerLookup`	This lookup class is recommended if you are running your application in the JBoss Application Server, and works with JBoss AS versions 4 through to 7.
`JBossStandaloneJTAManagerLookup`	If you are not running within a Java EE environment and still wish to use JTA transactions, we recommend using JBoss Transactions—a fast, powerful JTA transaction manager that can be run standalone, outside of a Java EE environment. This lookup class has the ability to attach to a standalone instance of JBoss Transactions.

If no transaction lookup class is specified, `org.infinispan.transaction.lookup.GenericTransactionManagerLookup` will be used by default. This lookup class is capable of locating the Transaction Manager in most popular Java EE application servers; however, it defaults to `DummyTransactionManagerLookup` if no Transaction Manager is found.

The transactional mode can be either **TRANSACTIONAL** or **NON_TRANSACTIONAL**. By default, all caches are accessed non-transactionally, which means that the operations executed on a cache do not start or join any JTA transaction.

The `lockingMode` attribute controls how locks are acquired on the cache. Locks are the mechanism used by Infinispan to coordinate concurrent writes to entries, and to prevent problems such as data corruption that may arise from simultaneous updates.

The default locking mode is **Optimistic**, which defers lock acquisition to transaction *prepare* time.

As you can see from the following diagram, when the transaction's initiator issues a request to commit the transaction, it starts the first phase of the two-phase commit protocol by querying—via prepare messages—to all participants whether to abort or to commit the transaction. It is in this phase that locks are acquired on each member in the cluster.

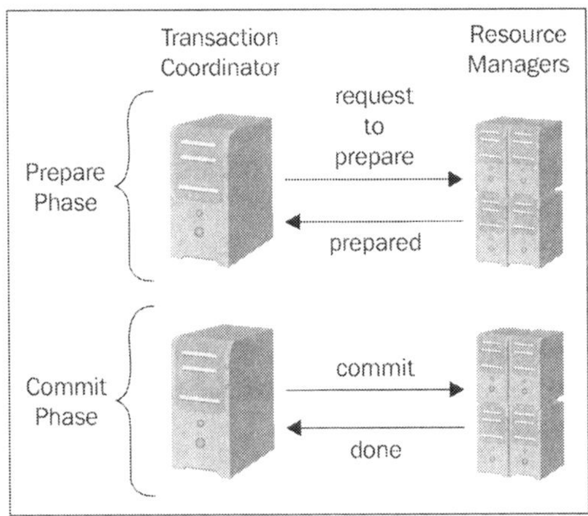

If all participants vote to commit, the transaction's initiator informs all the participants to commit their share of the transaction by sending a commit message in the second phase.

The advantage of using this locking model is the reduced duration for which locks are held, and increased throughput; deadlocks can also be dealt with using lock reordering and deadlock detection. However, there is a possibility that transactions may fail and be forced to roll back—such as in the event of being unable to acquire a lock in time or the existence of a deadlock.

On the other hand, with **Pessimistic** locking, locks are acquired on each update operation, in an eager fashion. Thus, when a cache updates one entry, it will block another write on the same entry from the time the update happens through to the time the transaction completes—regardless of whether the transaction succeeds or aborts. Cache reads, however, do not block concurrent reads or writes, as the following code example shows:

```
transactionManager.begin();
cache.put(k1,v1); //k1 is locked
cache.remove(k2); //k2 is locked when this returns
transactionManager.commit();
```

When `cache.put(k1,v1)` returns, `k1` is locked and no other transaction can write to it. Reading `k1` is still possible. The lock on `k1` is released in the last line, which commits, and thus the transaction completes (`commit` or `rollback`).

Choosing between pessimistic and optimistic locking

From a use case perspective, optimistic locking should be used when there's not a lot of contention between multiple transactions running at the same time. That is because the optimistically locked transactions roll back if data has changed between the time it was read and the time it was committed, if `writeSkewCheck` is enabled.

On the other hand, pessimistically locked transactions are more costly by their nature, as each `write` operation potentially involves an RPC for lock acquisition. For this reason, pessimistic locking might be a better fit when there are a large number of threads updating the same entries, and transaction rollbacks/retries cannot be dealt with. Applications using pessimistic locking tend to hold locks for longer duration, and will result in a decreased throughput.

Explicit and implicit data locking

As we just said, Infinispan by default uses optimistic locking in a cluster, which delays lock acquisition to prepare time. You can, however, configure Infinispan to use pessimistic locking, which acquires locks eagerly. If you are using pessimistic locking, you can also make use of the lock method on the Cache API. As shown in the following example, you can gain fine-grained control of when locks are acquired, within the scope of your transaction:

```
tx.begin()
cache.lock(K1, K2) // acquire cluster wide lock on K1 and K2 cache.put
(K1,V1)  // guaranteed to succeed
cache.put(K2, V2) // also guaranteed to succeed
tx.commit() // release lock
```

Showing a node locking example

In this example, we will show how to use the `PESSIMISTIC` node locking, by creating the following sample configuration:

```
<namedCache name="transactional">

  <transaction
          transactionManagerLookupClass=
              "org.infinispan.transaction.lookup
              .GenericTransactionManagerLookup"
      transactionManagerLookupClass
      lockingMode="PESSIMISTIC"/>

</namedCache>
```

As far as our code is concerned, we will add a small addition to our Ticket Booking example, which includes the use case of a customer who wants to change a show booking:

```
DefaultCacheManager manager = null;
Cache<Integer, Ticket> cache = null;

public void start()  {
       manager = new DefaultCacheManager("cluster.xml");
       cache = m.getCache("transactional");

   while (true){
     . . . .
     else if (command.equals("change")) {

       String id = IOUtils.readLine("Enter Ticketid ");
       String show = IOUtils.readLine("Enter show ");

       Ticket ticket = cache.get(Integer.parseInt(id));
       ticket.setShow(show);
       beginTransaction();

       cache.put(Integer.parseInt(id), ticket);
       String captcha =
      UUID.randomUUID().toString().substring(0,4);
       String check =
      IOUtils.readLine("Enter captcha "+captcha);
       if (captcha.equals(check)) {
         commitTransaction();
         log("Updated ticket "+ticket);
       }
       else {
         rollbackTransaction();
         log("Updated failed!");
```

```
            }
        }
         // other options stays the same
    }
    public void beginTransaction() {
            cache.getAdvancedCache().
               getTransactionManager().begin();
    }
    public void commitTransaction() {
            cache.getAdvancedCache().
               getTransactionManager().commit();
    }
    public void rollbackTransaction() {
            cache.getAdvancedCache().
               getTransactionManager().rollback();
    }
```

As you can see from this example, the `TransactionManager` interface is acquired via an internal Infinispan API. Please bear in mind that in a Java EE environment, the portable and correct way to define transaction boundaries is via the **UserTransaction** interface, which can be conveniently injected as a **Resource** (See *Chapter 2, Using Infinispan Core API,* for an example of it). Use Infinispan's Advanced Cache just for testing and demonstration purposes, as in the earlier mentioned example.

The rest of the code is pretty much the same, the only update being the addition to our command-line interface of the command `change`, which allows modification of the show booking. The `change` command also includes a `captcha` test, which will allow concurrent changes to the same entry by another transaction.

Now, start two Eclipse consoles (or two basic command-line consoles):

1. In any one of these two consoles, book a ticket first. Because this operation has not been included in a JTA transaction, it should immediately be visible to the other JVMs consoles, also.
2. Now comes the tricky part; send a `change` command for "ticket 1" and do not enter the `captcha` code as yet. At this point, we have locked the entry with "key 1", but no commit has yet been issued.

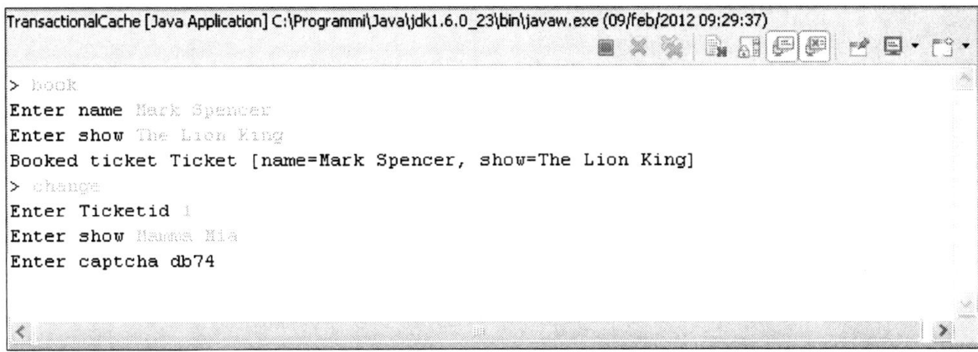

3. In the other console, we will try to pay the ticket by issuing the `pay` command. This will result in an entry being removed, which will be deferred until the lock on that entry is released.

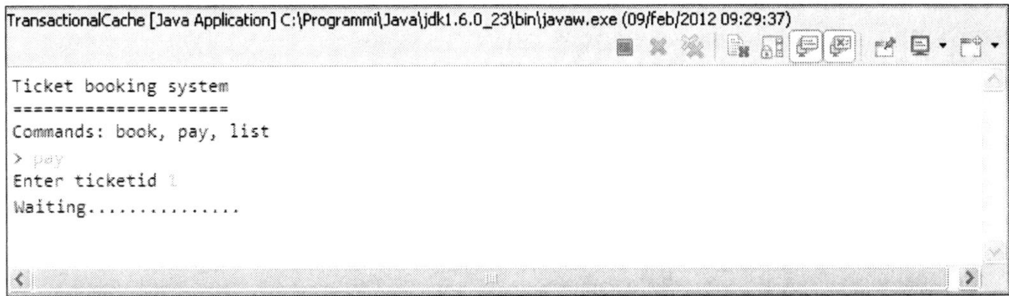

4. Now, return to the first console and fill up the `captcha` code. The transaction will commit (or rollback, if you fail to enter the `captcha` code correctly).

```
TransactionalCache [Java Application] C:\Programmi\Java\jdk1.6.0_23\bin\javaw.exe (09/feb/2012 09:29:37)
> book
Enter name Mark Spencer
Enter show The Lion King
Booked ticket Ticket [name=Mark Spencer, show=The Lion King]
> change
Enter Ticketid 1
Enter show Mamma Mia
Enter captcha db74db74
```

5. Verify that the second console has been unlocked and, thus, the entry removed.

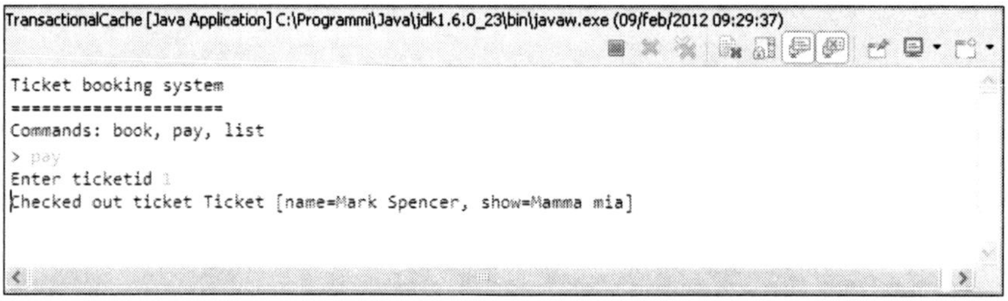

```
TransactionalCache [Java Application] C:\Programmi\Java\jdk1.6.0_23\bin\javaw.exe (09/feb/2012 09:29:37)
Ticket booking system
=====================
Commands: book, pay, list
> pay
Enter ticketid 1
Checked out ticket Ticket [name=Mark Spencer, show=Mamma mia]
```

Configuring lock timeouts

If you have been able to complete the previous sample without any error, it means that you are a super-fast at data entry! Actually, if you leave the default lock policies, it's likely that a timeout was encountered as the second console was unable to acquire a lock in the default timeout, which is 10 seconds:

```
Exception in thread "main" org.infinispan.util.concurrent.
TimeoutException: Unable to acquire lock after [10 seconds] on key [1]
for requestor [GlobalTransaction:<FRANCESCO-NB-30566>:1:remote]! Lock
held by [GlobalTransaction:<FRANCESCO-NB-6442>:1:local]
```

The lock timeout can be configured to a higher threshold, in the lock section of your default or named cache configuration. For example, if we expect transactions to hold on to locks for longer, then we should specify a higher lock acquisition timeout. In this case, lets set the lock acquisition timeout to 30 seconds:

```
<locking lockAcquisitionTimeout="30000"/>
```

Using lock pools to guard your cache keys

By default, Infinispan creates a lock per entry in the cache. In a highly concurrent environment, you can however take advantage of a feature called **lock striping** (disabled by default), which consists of a pool of shared locks that is maintained for all entries that need to be locked.

By using lock striping, you will benefit from better memory utilization as locks take up a lot of memory. This, however, can sometimes lead to deadlocks, if locks for different keys end up in the same lock stripe, and can also reduce concurrent throughput if the pool of locks isn't large enough.

As we said, by default, lock striping is disabled. However, if you think that the advantage of better memory utilization exceeds the risk of potential deadlocks, you can enable this feature by setting `useLockStriping` to `true`, in the `locking` section:

```
<locking useLockStriping="true"/>
```

Detecting deadlocks

Deadlock detection is a prevention mechanism aimed at optimistically locked configurations, where reordering of locks for a given transaction can take place at prepare time. Infinispan is able to detect any deadlock on enabling the `deadLockDetection` element in your configuration:

```
<deadlockDetection enabled="true" spinDuration="1000"/>
```

The `spingDuration` parameter determines how often (in milliseconds) lock acquisition is attempted within the maximum time allowed to acquire a particular lock.

Detecting deadlocks can, however, impact the performance of your applications as sleeping threads need to frequently wake up and check its status with the deadlock detection manager. This can be a context switching overhead, so you should carefully evaluate and benchmark the configuration before enabling it in a production system. The most obvious clue that you might have a deadlock problem is a high number of `TimeoutException` errors thrown by your applications. In the next chapter, which is about monitoring Infinispan, we will investigate how to monitor your transaction statistics.

Summary

In this chapter, we have seen some advanced topics that are usually connected with clustered applications. Each clustered application needs a network transport that is used to move messages to the other members of the cluster. Infinispan uses the JGroups toolkit library as its backbone for data transmission, letting you choose the protocol type used for communication (TCP or UDP) and even to customize the protocol stack.

Next, we demonstrated how to turn our Ticket Booking example into a clustered one, by providing a simple, clustered configuration.

Infinispan offers three clustering modes to share data between nodes: Replication means that the data contained in each node is replicated across all other nodes of the cluster. Distribution aims to distribute data efficiently across a set of nodes using advanced algorithms to store and retrieve the data, and Invalidation allows you to maintain cluster-aware "local" caches that are able to invalidate entries if entries are modified elsewhere in the cluster.

Then, we covered some advanced insights related to JTA transactions. By using transactions, you can include your cache operations a as part of an ongoing transaction. We also explored some of the details around locking of entries within a transaction.

Having learned the basic and advanced configuration settings, we will now explore how we can monitor the status of your data grid. That's the goal of the next chapter.

5
Monitoring Infinispan

This chapter dives into management and monitoring Infinispan, showing you how to collect runtime information and statistics on the cache manager and cache instances.

In the coming sections, we will first show how to enable the collection of statistics; then, we will show two tools that can be used to collect and manage this data:

- The JConsole application, which ships with the JDK
- The RHQ web-based management platform

Enabling statistics collection

Infinispan uses **Java Management Extensions** (**JMX**) to expose management operations and statistical data. By default, statistics are not enabled.

In order to enable them, you first need to add the `globalJmxStatistics` element within the global section, as follows:

```
<global>
   <globalJmxStatistics enabled="true"/>
</global>
```

This element specifies that global statistics are gathered and reported via JMX for all caches under this cache manager. Statistics can also be enabled at cache level; just use the `jmxStatistics` element, either in the `default` or `namedCache` elements, as follows:

```
<jmxStatistics enabled="true"/>
```

Once you have enabled JMX Statistics, you can choose your favorite tool to collect and manage data.

Using JConsole to gather Infinispan data

The first tool we will show in this book is **JConsole**, which is a JMX-compliant monitoring tool that is built in with the J2SE distribution. JConsole uses the extensive JMX instrumentation of the Java virtual machine, to provide information on performance and resource consumption of the JVM itself, in addition to applications running within the JVM.

The command syntax to start JConsole for local monitoring is as follows:

```
jconsole [processID]
```

(Here, `processID` is the application's process ID (PID)).

Windows users can simply execute the `jconsole.exe` file, which is located in the `bin` folder of the J2SE distribution.

The JConsole interface is composed of six tabs:

- **Summary**: This tab displays summary information about the JVM and monitored values
- **Memory**: This displays information about memory use
- **Threads**: This displays information about thread use
- **Classes**: This tab displays information about class loading
- **MBeans**: This displays information about MBeans
- **VM**: This tab displays information about the JVM

We are mostly interested in the **MBean** tab, which displays information on all the MBeans registered with the platform MBean server. So, let's build up a concrete example of a cluster composed of four nodes, which uses the default GUI Demo settings:

```
<infinispan
      xmlns:xsi=
        "http://www.w3.org/2001/XMLSchema-instance"
      xsi:schemaLocation=
        "urn:infinispan:config:5.1
        http://www.infinispan.org/schemas/infinispan-config-5.1.xsd"
      xmlns="urn:infinispan:config:5.1">

    <global>
      <transport clusterName="demoCluster"/>
      <globalJmxStatistics enabled="true"/>
    </global>

    <default>
```

```
        <jmxStatistics enabled="true"/>
        <clustering mode="distribution">
            <l1 enabled="true"
              lifespan="60000"/>
            <hash numOwners="2"
              rehashRpcTimeout="120000"/>
            <sync/>
        </clustering>
    </default>
</infinispan>
```

As you can see from the following screenshot, the JConsole GUI contains the tree of MBeans on the left; they are organized according to their `objectNames`. When you select an MBean in the tree, its attributes, operations, notifications, and other information is displayed on the central panel:

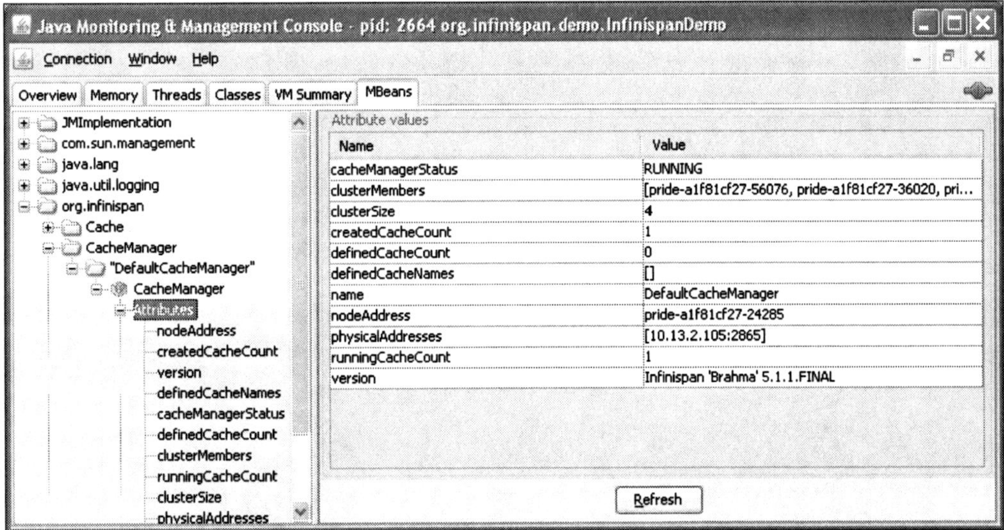

By expanding into the `org.infinispan` folder, you can find both the **Cache** and **CacheManager** nodes. Inside the **CacheManager** node, you will find (in the **Attributes** section) the most relevant cluster statistical data, such as cluster size, cluster members, the running caches count, and more.

Inside the **Cache** folder, you can find information that is related to specific cache instances that are running in the cluster. For example, in the **Statistics** subfolder, you can find comprehensive statistical information about cache operations. By inspecting these values, you can determine critical information, such as the cache hits and misses (a cache hit is a read operation fulfilled with a local or neighboring call; a cache miss is a read operation fulfilled resorting to a cache store), the average read/write time, or the number of entries evicted from the cache:

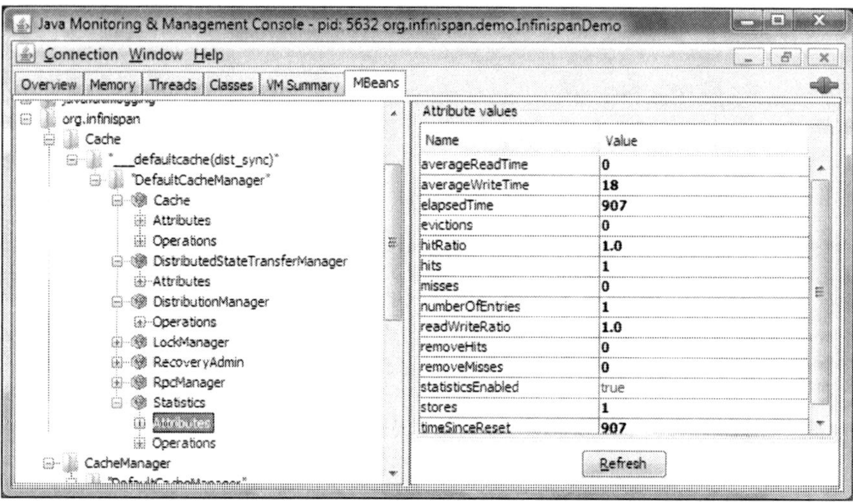

If you are going to use a clustered cache, the **RpcManager** MBean should be of interest to you, as it displays the statistics connected with communication between cluster members:

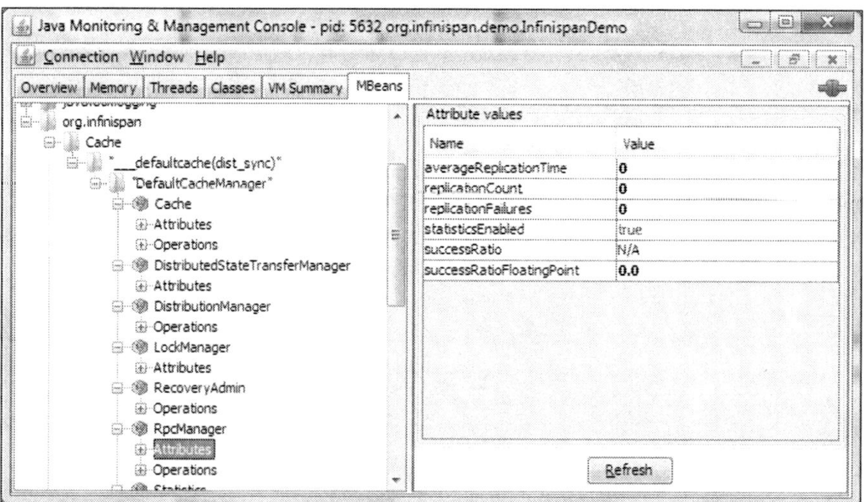

So far, we have seen how to collect data using the **MBeans** tab GUI; however, Infinispan MBeans not only provide read-only views of your cache, but also let you invoke operations on it. For example, under the **DistributionManager** subfolder, you can find out how your entries are distributed across the cluster, using the **locateKey** operation. In our example, we are using a distributed cache mode with `numOwners = 2`. Thus, each entry is distributed across two nodes of the cluster, as shown by the following picture:

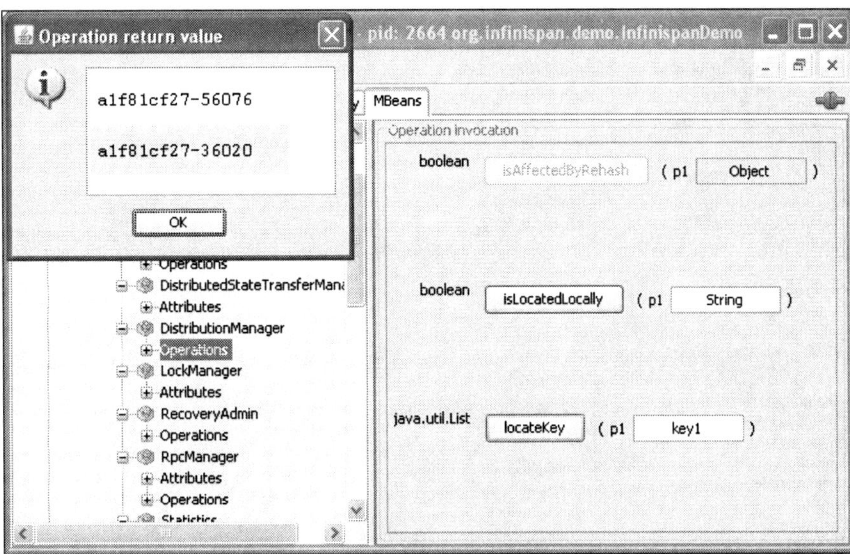

If you are using JTA transactions and have enabled transaction recovery, more advanced operations are found in the **RecoveryAdmin** MBean, which allows forcing commit or rollback of **in-doubt transactions**. In-doubt transactions are the result of a failure during a distributed transaction between Infinispan and another JTA resource such as the database. It can happen that both the JTA resources complete the **prepare phase** successfully for commit; however, only one resource is able to successfully respond to the commit phase, leaving the transaction in an indeterminate state.

In such a case, there will be an inconsistency between the various JTA resources and Infinispan, which will need reconciling.

Such a scenario is handled by a JTA transaction phase known as **Recovery**, which is able to detect in-doubt transactions, provided that it's enabled in the configuration:

```
<transaction
  useEagerLocking="true"
  eagerLockSingleNode="true">
    <recovery enabled="true" />
</transaction>
```

The Recovery process needs to be completed manually by a system administrator, using the operations that are located in the **RecoveryAdmin** MBean.

In-doubt transactions are shown by the `showInDoubtTransactions` operations, which will display the transactions, XID related to the transactions, Infinispan's internal ID, and the transaction status.

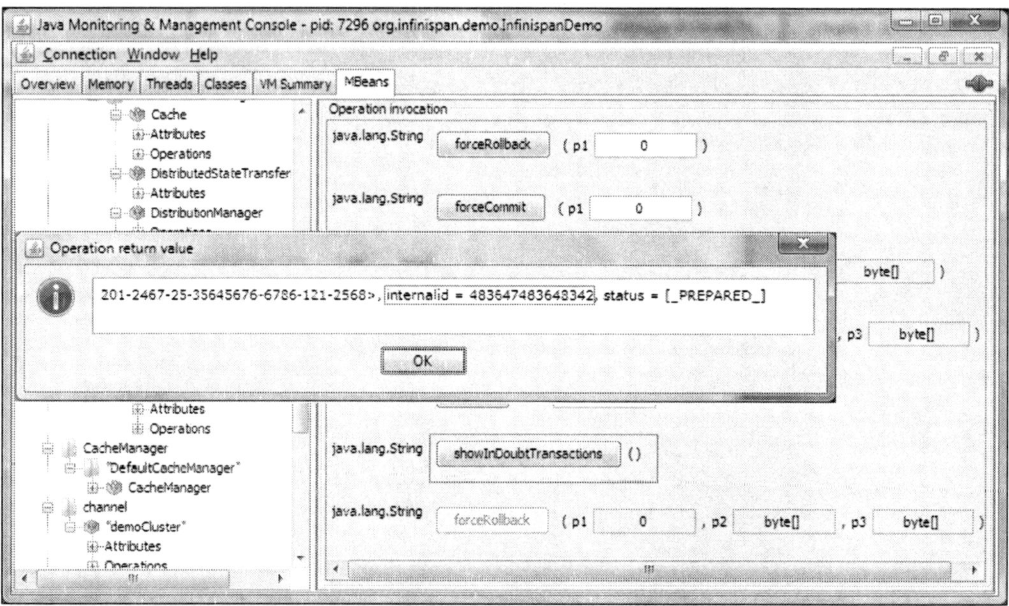

In order to complete the transaction, the `internalid` attribute of the transaction needs to be passed as an argument to the `forceRollback` or `forceCommit` operations, thus solving the conflict between JTA resources.

Managing Infinispan with RHQ

Although JConsole provides a simple way to collect statistics and manage Infinispan platform, the most advanced way to manage multiple Infinispan instances spread across different servers is to use RHQ. RHQ is an open source management and monitoring platform that, thanks to its agent and auto-discovery capabilities, makes monitoring multiple Cache Manager and Cache instances across a cluster a very simple task.

Under the hood, RHQ is designed with layered modules that provide a flexible architecture for deployment. It delivers a core user interface that delivers audited and historical data of your application.

Here, we will provide a quick installation tour of it; should you need further details, we suggest you look at the installation guide, which can be located at `http://support.rhq-project.org/display/JOPR2/Installation`.

Installing RHQ

In order to install RHQ, you basically need a Linux, Windows, or Mac OSX operating system, and an x86_64, i686, or ia64 processor. Then, RHQ requires Java 6 or higher, in order to run both the RHQ Server and the RHQ Agent.

1. The first step will be downloading RHQ. So, go to the download page located at `http://support.rhq-project.org/display/RHQ/Download`, and download the latest stable release (at the time of writing, this was `rhq-server-4.2.0.zip`)
2. With your favorite zip tool, unzip the **RHQ Server** distribution file to the directory from within which it will be executed:

   ```
   unzip rhq-server-*.zip
   ```

3. Now start the RHQ Server:
   - For UNIX, execute the following:

     ```
     cd <server-install-dir>/bin
     ./rhq-server.sh start
     ```

   - For Windows, you can opt to install RHQ as a service by executing the following from the command line:

     ```
     cd <server-install-dir>/bin
     rhq-server.bat install
     ```

   Once installed, you can start the server in the same way we did with the Unix operating system:

   ```
   rhq-server.bat start
   ```

4. The RHQ Server process will start in the background, as displayed in the following screenshot:

5. Now point your browser to `http://localhost:7080/`. Because the RHQ Server has not completed its installation yet, this URL will take you to the RHQ Server Installer web application.

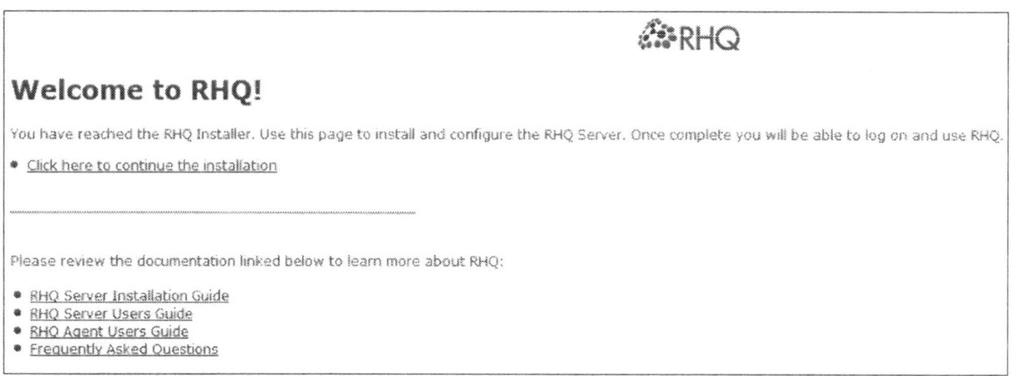

By default, the installer displays only the basic settings required for installation. If you're just building a demo or testing the RHQ server, you can avoid the need to install a fully-fledged database and can use an in-memory H2 database instead.

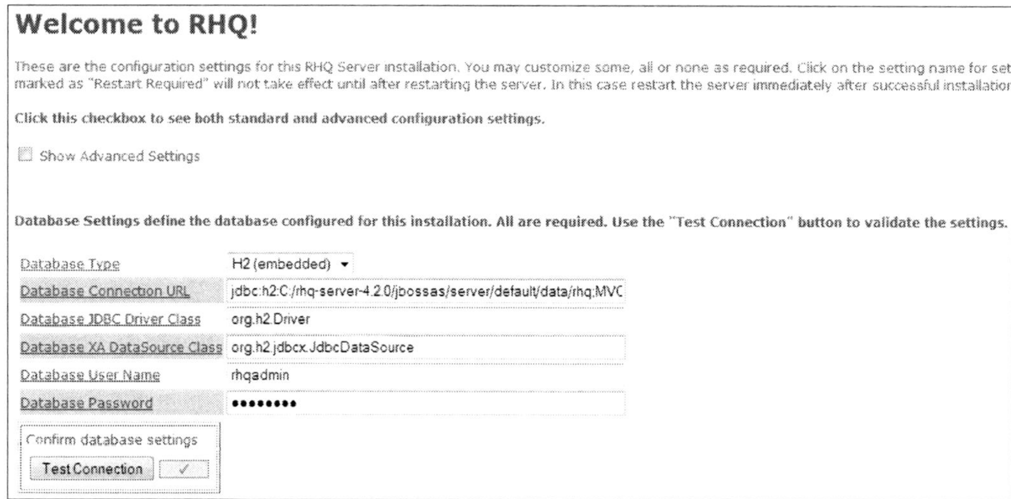

Once you have learnt the basics of RHQ, you are encouraged to switch to PostGres or Oracle DB. See this paper for more information: `http://rhq-project.org/display/JOPR2/Running+The+Installer`.

When you have successfully tested your DB connection, you can save your settings and finish the installation.

Configuring the RHQ agent

In order to collect data from your services, an agent needs to be installed on each of the machines being monitored. The most common setup is to have the RHQ agent installed on the same machine on which Infinispan is running. If you have multiple machines, an agent can be installed on each machine.

However, if you want to get started quickly with RHQ, you can simply activate the embedded agent that ships with the RHQ distribution. In order to activate the embedded agent, find `rhq-server-properties`, which is located in the `bin` folder of your RHQ distribution, and enable it by changing the following property (it should be located around line 105 of the configuration file):

```
# Embedded RHQ Agent
rhq.server.embedded-agent.enabled=true
```

Letting the agent discover Infinispan

The RHQ agent will automatically be able to detect running Infinispan instances.

However, certain older versions of Infinispan are not able to automatically get detected by RHQ, and you will need to set some properties, as follows, to make sure that RHQ agents are able to discover Infinispan instances:

- `-Dcom.sun.management.jmxremote.port=6996`
- `-Dcom.sun.management.jmxremote.ssl=false`
- `-Dcom.sun.management.jmxremote.authenticate=false`

These properties need to be set on the JVM that runs Infinispan; for example, if you are going to use the GUI demo, just include these properties within the `runGUIDemo` script. If, on the other hand, you are planning to use Infinispan embedded into JBoss AS 7, consider setting these properties into the `standalone/domain` script (read more about Infinispan and AS 7 integration in *Appendix, Infinispan and JBoss AS 7*).

Installing the Infinispan plugin

The RHQ platform is a modular infrastructure that is able to capture a large set of events by simply installing the required plugins. The Infinispan plugin is not included by default in the RHQ installation, so you have to import it. However, that's a very simple task that can be completed through the RHQ GUI.

1. Let's connect to the RHQ Server from your browser at the following address, which will direct you into the site dashboard: `http://localhost:7080/Dashboard.do`.
2. A login form will be prompted; you can use the default credentials, which are `rhqadmin/rhqadmin`:

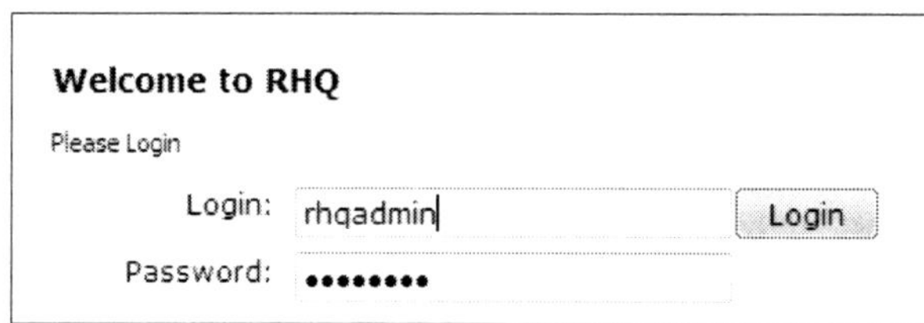

3. The RHQ dashboard will be displayed, showing all the resources that have been committed, or the new ones that have been discovered. In our example, the RHQ Server has detected your operating system with a set of services running on it (basically the RHQ Server itself is a JBoss AS instance that has been discovered by the agent):

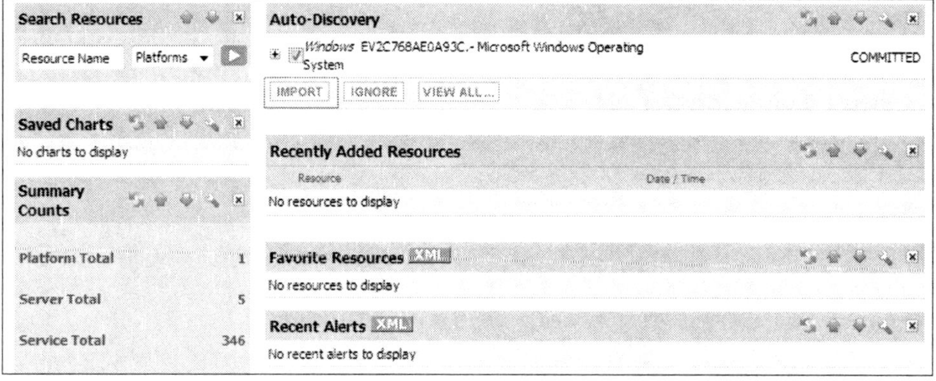

4. Once the resources have been imported, you will be moved to the main application window that controls all your resources. Move to the **Administration** tab and select **Agent Plugins** from the **Configuration** tab on the left:

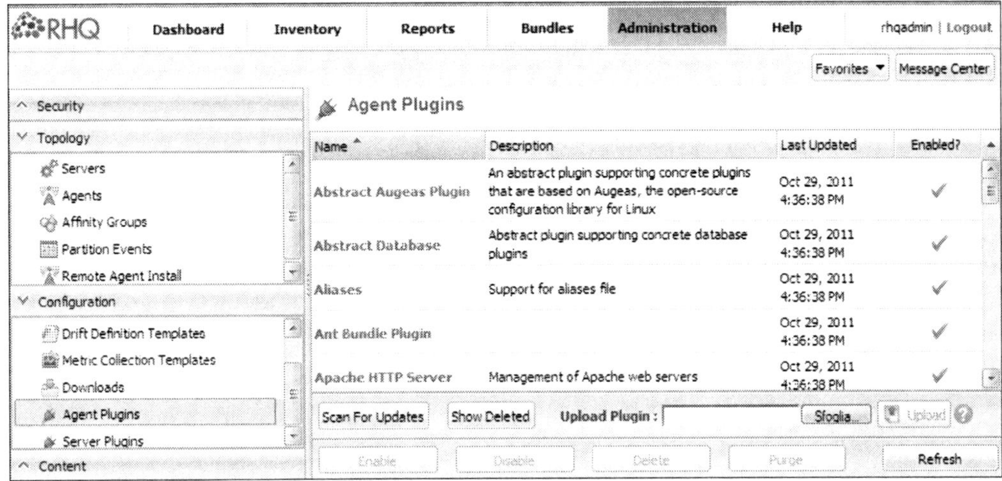

5. In the **Upload Plugin** area below, choose the Infinispan plugin, which should be named something like `infinispan-rhq-plugin.jar`, located under the `modules/rhq-plugin` directory of your Infinispan distribution:

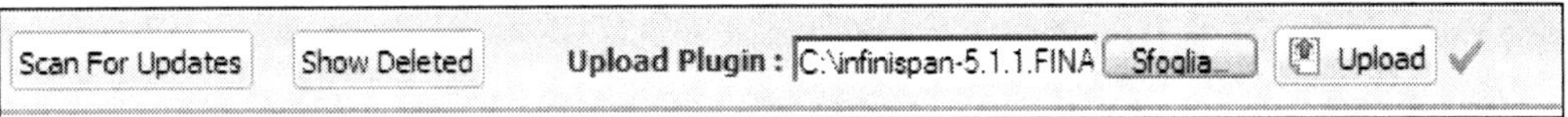

6. Now that the installation phase is complete, return to the dashboard window and verify that RHQ has successfully discovered Infinispan JMX MBeans:

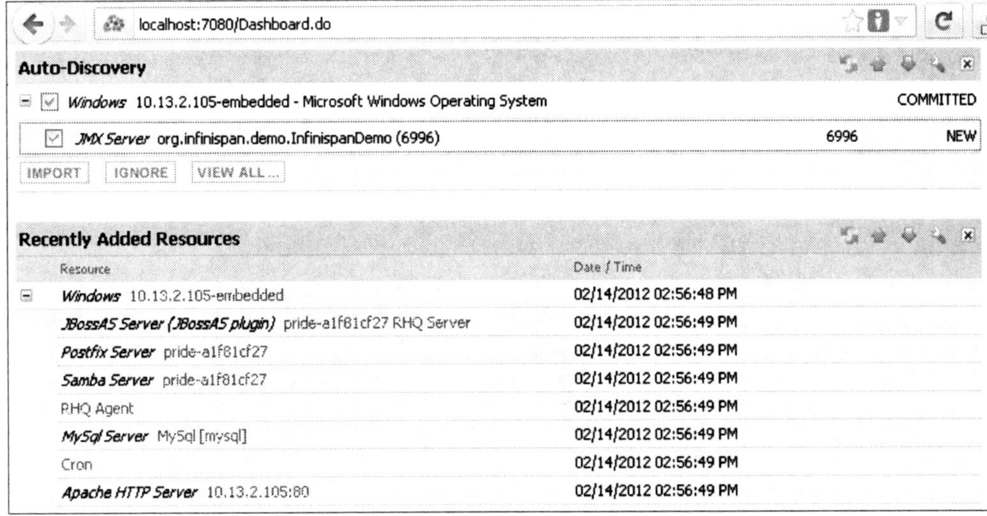

7. Now, choose to import the new resources and you are ready to monitor every bit of your Infinispan server!

RHQ: your gateway to Infinispan

The installation procedure was a bit long to complete, however, you will soon realize that it was worthwhile. From the **Inventory** tab menu, you can inspect all the resources available in your system. To be precise, on the left-hand side of the screen, your resources are organized in a tree-like structure. In the middle of the page, you can manage the resource that is selected in your tree:

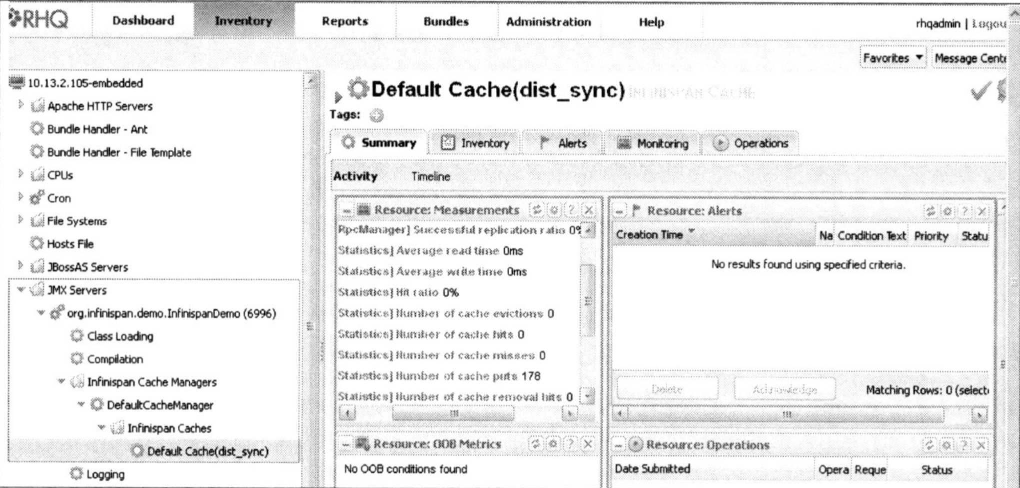

In our case, we will inspect under the **JMX Servers** folder where Infinispan servers should be located. Select the **Default Cache** element and shift your attention to the center of the page. Every resource selected can be examined through the following tabs:

- **Summary**: This tab displays general statistics about the selected resource. In our example, selecting the **Default Cache** will display the same general Cache statistics we have seen earlier via JConsole.
- **Inventory**: This tab acts as central repository for items that are a part of the resource which houses items managed and monitored by RHQ. Before an item can take advantage of the feature set that RHQ provides, it must first be imported into the inventory.

- **Alert**: This tab can be used to provide some form of auditing data telling you that one or more conditions were true at the time it fired; it also specifies which parties need to be notified at that time.
- **Monitoring**: This tab contains centralized scheduling control and a collection of information attached to resources.
- **Operations**: This tab is about executing some features or functions against resources in the inventory.

When combined, all the aforementioned options can really produce a wealth of information about your subsystem that is being monitored. Detailing all the capabilities of this platform would require a book of its own; however, in the next few pages we will whet your appetite with some highlights. Please refer to the official documentation (`http://www.rhq-project.org/display/JOPR2/Home`) if you want to learn more.

A quick Summary view of our cache

The **Summary** view provides a precise measurement of your cache-sensitive data with both numerical and statistical information. This should be your first stop when you need to gather information about your cache.

Within the **Summary** view, we can check the **Resource** portlet, which contains raw statistics about your cache, along with a tiny graphical view of them:

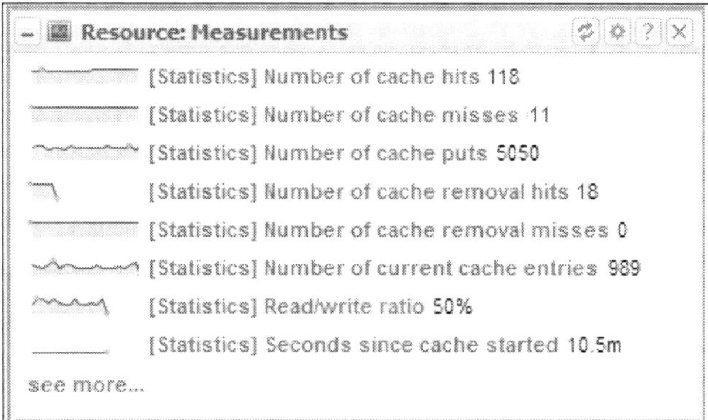

Besides the data, this portlet contains a set of buttons that allow you to refresh the data (1st button), to choose a time frame for your data collection (2nd button), to get information about the portlet (3rd button), or to close it (5th button).

By clicking on the single resource, you can zoom in on the graphical detail of the resource, which shows the trend of the data through time, including peak, average, and low metrics:

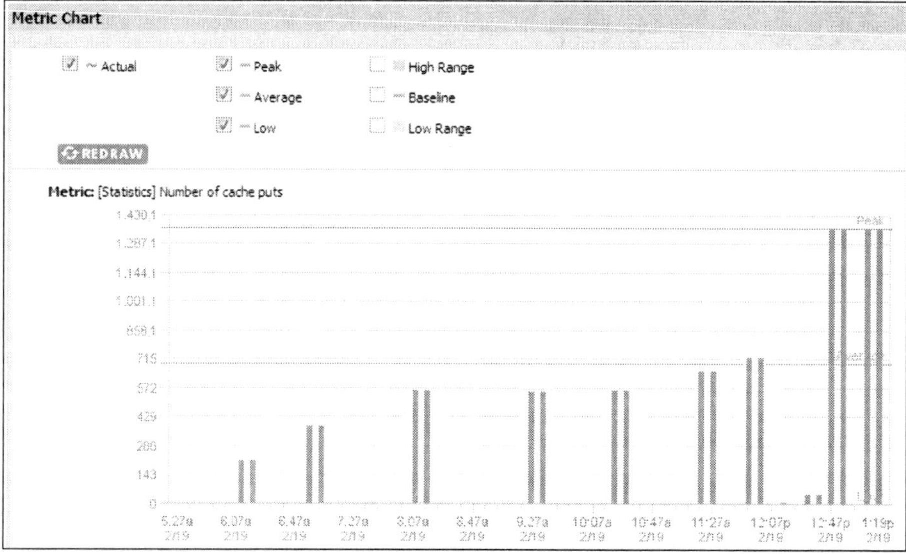

Getting alert conditions from your cache

The **alerts** subsystem provides a variety of different options for being notified about potential issues in the system. Each resource in the inventory may have zero or many alert definitions. The condition is set at the heart of the alert definition. By selecting the **Conditions** tab of your alert subsystem, we will be able to add or delete an alert condition:

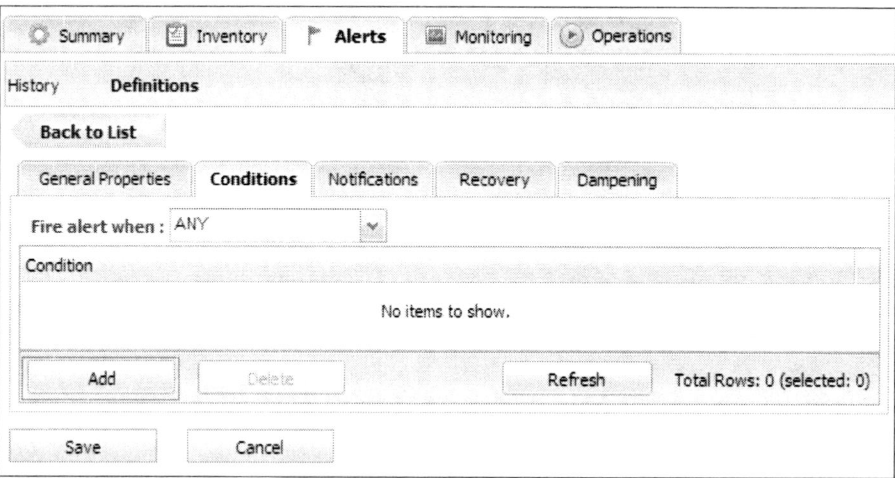

An alert condition can be based on a set of different condition types and metrics. In this example, we will add an alert that fires when the number of caches exceeds 200 units (this will make it fairly easy to test this metric, if you are running the GUI Demo):

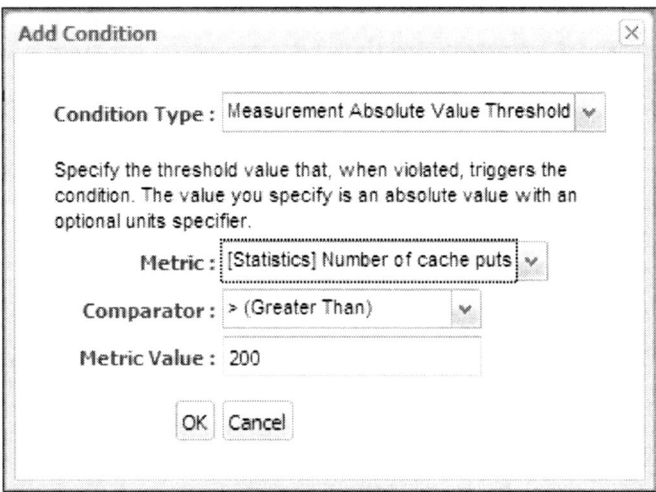

Now start adding some data in your cache from your Infinispan API or GUI Demo, and move back to the **Summary** view. In a matter of minutes, you will see our sample alert pumping up, as and when the condition is met:

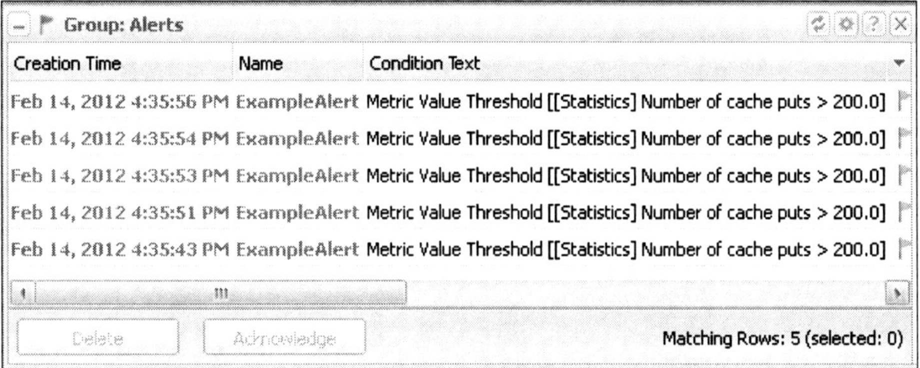

This is the most basic way to acknowledge a system metric. You can get different types of notifications (such as e-mail to users or groups) by digging into the **Alert Notifications** menu. You can also refine your metrics through the **Dampening alert** menu, which allows limiting the occurrences or time period of a particular metric. As you can see, the capabilities of this framework are countless, but unfortunately, there is not enough room in this book to illustrate them all.

Monitoring your system in real time

The **monitoring** subsystem is one of the richest areas of RHQ toolkit. Monitoring is primarily concerned with gathering data (called metrics or measurements) from each of the resources in inventory. By default, data is shown in graphical format; you can, however, choose to present them in tabular form, and even show side-by-side comparisons of the current or historic values, between various metrics across different resources.

Let's click on the **Monitoring** tab, so that you can quickly see the real-time statistics of the attributes that are able to emit JMX metrics (we have already mentioned them in the *A quick Summary view of our cache* section):

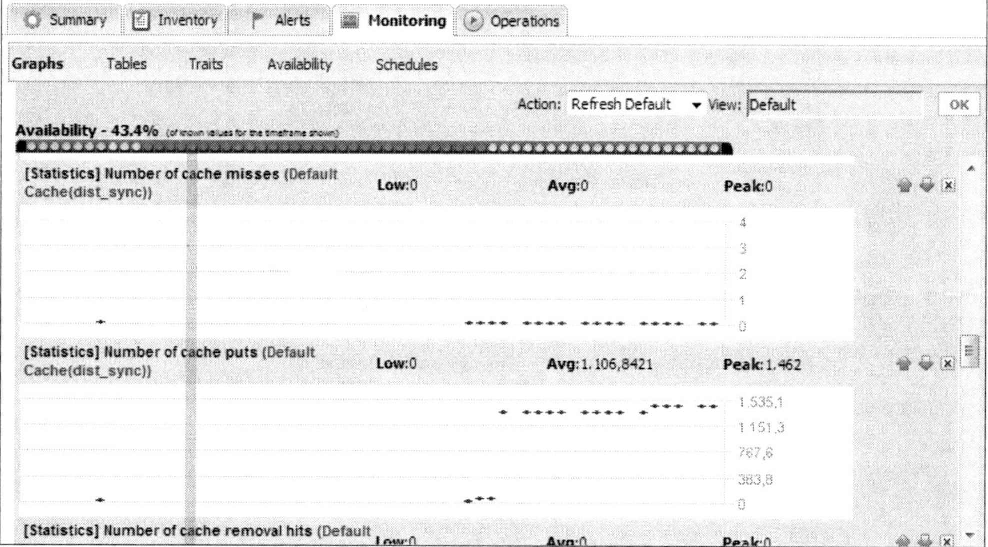

As you can see from the previous graph, the monitoring subsystem provides running baselines to show metrics that go out of their normal ranges, and also the availability of resources during the selected time frame.

The very nature of numerical data makes it easy to graph and provide visual history for changes to the values, over time; RHQ calls these metrics. String-based data, on the other hand, is better represented as a list of changes to the value of that string over time; RHQ calls these traits.

A typical example of a trait is the cache status, which can be monitored by switching to the **Traits** submenu:

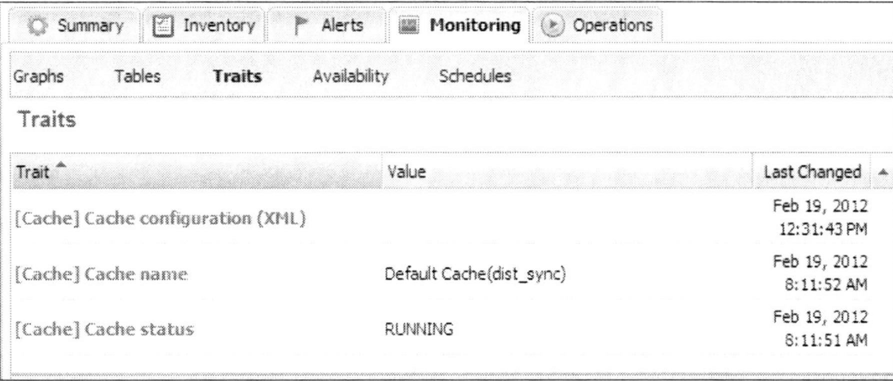

Summary

In this chapter, we have focused on collecting statistics and managing your Infinispan resources. Infinispan uses JMX to expose and manage runtime data; however, by default no statistics are delivered until you enable them either at the CacheManager level, or at the Cache level.

Once your Infinispan cache statistics are enabled, you can use any instrument that is able to connect to Infinispan MBeans. In particular, we have looked at how to use JConsole and RHQ.

6
Infinispan and CDI

Contexts and Dependency Injection, often abbreviated to **CDI**, is a programming model for enterprise Java that is fast gaining popularity. It is available as a standalone framework, but is also included in the **Java Enterprise Edition version 6** (**Java EE 6**) specification.

As such, it was considered important for developers to be able to make use of Infinispan through CDI.

A 30,000 foot overview of CDI

At its core, CDI is an annotation-driven injection framework that minimizes the bulk of boilerplate code that developers have to write. It is designed to greatly increase productivity, testability, and the quality of business applications built on the Java platform. Any Java EE 6-compliant application server has the ability to deploy a CDI application.

To many, CDI is an "official" version of the popular Spring Framework, which not only modernizes some of the concepts popularized by Spring, but also standardizes them and bakes them into the core of enterprise Java—Java EE.

To learn more about CDI, visit the Weld website (`http://sfwk.org/Weld`). Weld is the reference implementation of the CDI specification.

This chapter assumes familiarity with CDI and does not attempt to introduce CDI basics. There are several excellent resources online about CDI, including the relevant sections in the official Java EE 6 tutorial (`http://docs.oracle.com/javaee/6/tutorial/doc/giwhb.html`).

In this chapter, we will:

- Get set up to use Infinispan in a CDI application
- Use CDI to configure and inject an Infinispan cache into your CDI application
- Use CDI to create caches using custom cache managers
- Use the JSR-107-compatible CDI annotations to reduce boilerplate code

Getting set up to use Infinispan and CDI

Infinispan provides an `infinispan-cdi` module that integrates Infinispan with CDI. If you are using Maven in your project, simply declare a dependency on `infinispan-cdi` in your Maven `pom.xml` file, as shown in the following code snippet:

```
<dependencies>
   ...
   <!—this declares a dependency on infinispan-cdi -->
   <dependency>
      <groupId>org.infinispan</groupId>
      <artifactId>infinispan-cdi</artifactId>
      <version>${version.infinispan}</version>
   </dependency>
   ...
</dependencies>
```

If you are not using Maven, the `infinispan-cdi` jar file and its dependencies are included in the zip distribution, under `modules/infinispan-cdi`.

Configuring and injecting Infinispan components into your CDI beans

This section discusses how you can configure and inject Infinispan components into your CDI beans.

Injecting a cache using CDI

CDI allows for components and services to be injected into your CDI components. An Infinispan cache is one such component that can be injected. The following code snippet injects a cache instance into your CDI component:

```
public class MyCDIComponent {
   @Inject
```

```
    Cache<String, String> cache;
}
```

Remote caches are supported as well. The following code snippet injects a remote cache instance, which connects to a cache server over the Hot Rod protocol:

```
public class MyCDIComponent {
    @Inject
    RemoteCache<String, String> remoteCache;
}
```

Configuring which cache gets injected

You can also create your own custom cache qualifier annotations, to return a specific cache using standard CDI annotations:

```
@javax.inject.Qualifier
@Target({ElementType.FIELD, ElementType.PARAMETER, ElementType.
METHOD})
@Retention(RetentionPolicy.RUNTIME)
@Documented
public @interface SmallCache {}
```

You can now specify how caches that are annotated with the `@SmallCache` qualifier are created:

```
import org.infinispan.configuration.cache.Configuration;
import org.infinispan.configuration.cache.ConfigurationBuilder;
import org.infinispan.cdi.ConfigureCache;
import javax.enterprise.inject.Produces;

public class CacheCreator {
    @ConfigureCache("smallcache") // This is the cache name.
    @SmallCache // This is the cache qualifier.
    @Produces
    public Configuration specialCacheCfg() {
        return new ConfigurationBuilder()
                    .eviction()
                        .strategy(EvictionStrategy.LRU)
                        .maxEntries(10)
                    .build();
    }
}
```

Now, with these two constructs (a qualifier annotation and a producer class), we can inject the specific cache into your CDI component, as follows:

```
public class MyCDIComponent {
   @Inject @SmallCache
   Cache<String, String> mySmallCache;
}
```

Configuring cache managers

Cache managers—both embedded and remote—can be configured using CDI as well.

Specifying the default configuration

Providing a method that is annotated as a producer for an Infinispan `Configuration` object means that this method is called whenever a default configuration is needed, as opposed to the default `Configuration` that is shipped with Infinispan:

```
public class Config {
    // By default CDI adds the @Default qualifier
    //if no other qualifier is provided.
    @Produces
    public Configuration defaultEmbeddedCacheConfiguration() {
        return new ConfigurationBuilder()
                    .eviction()
                        .strategy(EvictionStrategy.LRU)
                        .maxEntries(100)
                    .build();
    }
}
```

The `@Produces` annotation, placed on an arbitrary method that returns a `Configuration` instance, indicates that that method should be invoked whenever a `Configuration` object is needed. In this example, the contents of the method simply create a new `Configuration` object, configure it, and return it.

Overriding the way an EmbeddedCacheManager is created

Annotating a method as a producer for the `EmbeddedCacheManager` type allows you to override the way it is created, and a method annotated as such will be called the first time an `EmbeddedCacheManager` is required:

```
public class Config {

    @Produces
    // Restrict this custom producer to just your application
    @ApplicationScoped
    public EmbeddedCacheManager defaultEmbeddedCacheManager() {
      Configuration cfg = new ConfigurationBuilder()
            .eviction()
            .strategy(EvictionStrategy.LRU)
            .maxEntries(150)
            .build();
      return new DefaultCacheManager(cfg);
    }
}
```

The following example creates an `EmbeddedCacheManager` capable of creating clustered caches:

```
public class Config {

    @Produces
    @ApplicationScoped
    public EmbeddedCacheManager defaultClusteredCacheManager() {
        GlobalConfiguration g = new GlobalConfigurationBuilder()
                    .clusteredDefault()
                    .transport()
                    .clusterName("InfinispanCluster")
                    .build();
        Configuration cfg = new ConfigurationBuilder()
                    .eviction()
                    .strategy(EvictionStrategy.LRU)
                    .maxEntries(150)
                    .build();


         return new DefaultCacheManager(g, cfg);
    }
}
```

The `@Produces`-annotated method in the previous section generated `Configuration` objects, whereas the two `@Produces`-annotated methods in the aforementioned two examples generate `EmbeddedCacheManager` objects. So, if your code wanted to get a hold of a cache manager, you would simply do the following in your CDI bean, and the appropriate `@Produces`-annotated method will be invoked to generate `EmbeddedCacheManager` and inject this into your code at runtime:

```
...
@Inject
EmbeddedCacheManager cacheManager;
...
```

Configuring a RemoteCacheManager

`RemoteCacheManager` can be configured in a manner similar to configuring `EmbeddedCacheManager`, as discussed previously:

```
public class Config {
    @Produces
    @ApplicationScoped
    public RemoteCacheManager defaultRemoteCacheManager() {
      return new RemoteCacheManager(ADDRESS, PORT);
    }
}
```

Just as we saw before, the preceding code generates a `RemoteCacheManager` instead of an `EmbeddedCacheManager`.

Handling multiple configurations

You can have a single class configure multiple cache managers and remote cache managers, based on the qualifiers you create:

```
public class Config {
    @Produces
    @ApplicationScoped
    public EmbeddedCacheManager
      defaultEmbeddedCacheManager() {
        Configuration cfg = new ConfigurationBuilder()
                    .eviction()
                    .strategy(EvictionStrategy.LRU)
                    .maxEntries(150)
```

```
            .build();
        return new DefaultCacheManager(cfg);
    }

    @Produces
    @ApplicationScoped
    @ClusteredCache // A custom qualifier
    public EmbeddedCacheManager
      clusteredEmbeddedCacheManager() {
        Configuration cfg = new ConfigurationBuilder()
                    .eviction()
                    .strategy(EvictionStrategy.LRU)
                    .maxEntries(150)
            .build();
        return new DefaultCacheManager(cfg);
    }

    @Produces
    @ApplicationScoped
    public RemoteCacheManager
      defaultRemoteCacheManager() {
       return new RemoteCacheManager(ADDRESS, PORT);
   }

    @Produces
    @ApplicationScoped
    @RemoteCacheInDifferentDataCentre // A custom qualifier
    public RemoteCacheManager defaultRemoteCacheManager() {
       return new RemoteCacheManager(ADDRESS_FAR_AWAY, PORT);
    }
}
```

The aforementioned bean has the ability to produce several different types of cache managers— two different types of `EmbeddedCacheManager` and two different types of `RemoteCacheManager`. The appropriate method will be invoked when your application requests an `EmbeddedCacheManager` or a `RemoteCacheManager`, based on whether you ask for the default instance or one of the qualified instances. In this example, the two qualified instances are `@ClusteredCache` and `@RemoteCacheInDifferentDataCentre`.

Controlling storage and retrieval using CDI annotations

Some CDI annotations have been accepted into the JSR-107 (JCache) specification. All the annotations discussed in this section are a part of JSR-107 and are hence located in the `javax.cache` package.

These annotations provide value by intercepting method calls invoked on your CDI beans and performing storage and retrieval tasks in Infinispan as a side-effect.

Enabling cache annotations in your CDI application

All CDI applications have a `beans.xml` file. You need to edit your `beans.xml` file and add the following interceptors to your CDI `beans.xml` file, to enable method interception:

```
<beans xmlns="http://java.sun.com/xml/ns/javaee"
       xmlns:xsi="http://www.w3.org/2001/XMLSchema-instance"
       xsi:schemaLocation="http://java.sun.com/xml/ns/javaee http://
java.sun.com/xml/ns/javaee/beans_1_0.xsd">
  <interceptors>
      <class>
          org.infinispan.cdi.interceptor.CacheResultInterceptor
      </class>
      <class>
          org.infinispan.cdi.interceptor.CachePutInterceptor
      </class>
      <class>
          org.infinispan.cdi.interceptor.CacheRemoveEntryInterceptor
      </class>
      <class>
          org.infinispan.cdi.interceptor.CacheRemoveAllInterceptor
      </class>
  </interceptors>
</beans>
```

Caching the result of a method invocation

As mentioned before, CDI is all about productivity. As such, the common pattern of caching the result of an expensive operation is considered boilerplate. Consider the following case:

```
public String toCelsiusFormatted(float fahrenheit) {
    return
        NumberFormat.getInstance()
        .format((fahrenheit * 5 / 9) - 32)
        + " degrees Celsius";
}
```

A common pattern here would be to cache the result of this method call and to check the cache each time the result is needed. For example, the following code snippet is what one would typically do to look up the result of an expensive operation in a cache, perform the expensive operation in the event of a cache miss, and then cache the result again for future lookups:

```
float f = getTemperatureInFahrenheit();
Cache<Float, String>
    fahrenheitToCelsiusCache = getCache();
String celsius =
    fahrenheitToCelsiusCache.get(f);
if (celsius == null) {
    celsius = toCelsiusFormatted(f);
    fahrenheitToCelsiusCache.put(f, celsius);
}
```

CDI helps by eliminating all of the aforementioned boilerplate code, allowing you to simply annotate the method that generates data with the `@CacheResult` annotation:

```
@javax.cache.interceptor.CacheResult
public String toCelsiusFormatted(float fahrenheit) {
    return NumberFormat.getInstance()
      .format((fahrenheit * 5 / 9) - 32)
        + " degrees Celsius";
}
```

The annotation means that the CDI framework will first check the cache before actually executing the method, even though your code may invoke the call `toCelsiusFormatted()` directly. If the result already exists in the cache, this result is returned instead, and the method is not invoked at all.

Not all methods are suited to having their results cached. For example, results should always be new and (preferably) immutable objects, to prevent code changing values without consideration of other threads concurrently reading the same objects. Further, the way the cache is configured should be taken into account, as well. For example, reading from a cache that may result in a remote network lookup or deserialization from a cache loader may not be as cheap as expected, and sometimes the actual work done in the method could be cheaper.

While these statements are not specific to CDI annotations and apply to any of the cache APIs, they are particularly highlighted here as the CDI annotations make it trivial to cache the results of method calls with very little consideration given to certain side effects.

Specifying which cache to use

CDI allows you to do this too. The `@CacheResult` annotation takes an optional `cacheName` attribute:

```
@CacheResult(cacheName = "mySpecialCache")
public void doSomething(String parameter) { … }
```

Cache keys for cached results

The `@CacheResult` annotation creates a key for the result based on a combination of all the parameters on the method, by default. If you want more fine-grained control over which parameters form a part of this composite key, you would use the `@CacheKeyParam` annotation:

```
@CacheResult
public void doSomething
    (@CacheKeyParam String p1,
      @CacheKeyParam String p2,
      String dontCare) { … }
```

In the previous example, only `p1` and `p2` are considered when building the cache key. As such, repeated invocations of `doSomething()` with different values for the third parameter but the same values for the first and second parameters, will hit the cache and retrieve the same value.

Custom key generation

If you want to specify your own custom key generation scheme, you can override the default way in which the Infinispan-CDI module creates composite keys, by using the optional attribute of `@CacheResult` — `cacheKeyGenerator`:

```
@CacheResult(cacheKeyGenerator = MyCustomKeyGen.class)
public void doSomething(String p1, String p2){ … }
```

Removing an entry from the cache

When a method containing the `@CacheRemoveEntry` annotation is invoked, it causes the cache to remove an entry. The annotation takes an optional `cacheName` attribute, and an optional `cacheKeyGenerator` attribute, just like `@CacheResult`. Furthermore, method parameters can be annotated with `@CacheKeyParam`, as well:

```
@CacheRemoveEntry (cacheName = "cacheOfPeople")
public void changePersonName
    (@CacheKeyParam long personId,
    String newName) { … }
```

Clearing the cache

When a method containing the `@CacheRemoveAll` annotation is invoked, it causes the cache to be cleared. This annotation takes an optional `cacheName` attribute:

```
@CacheRemoveAll (cacheName = "statisticsCache")
public void resetStatistics() { … }
```

Updating a cache entry

When a method containing the `@CachePut` annotation is invoked, the parameter passed to the method annotated with `@CacheValue` is stored in the cache. `cacheName` and `cacheKeyGenerator` may optionally be specified on `@CachePut`, and some parameters on the invoked method may be annotated with `@CacheKeyParam`, to control key generation. The method is also invoked, as expected, in addition to the value being stored in the cache:

```
@CachePut (cacheName = "personCache")
public void updatePerson
    (@CacheKeyParam long personId,
    @CacheValue Person newPerson) { … }
```

For more details on the `@CacheResult`, `@CachePut`, `@CacheRemoveEntry`, and `@CacheRemoveAll` annotations, refer to the online API documentation for JSR-107 (JCache) at `http://jsr107.github.com/apidocs`.

Using Infinispan CDI with JBoss AS 7.x

JBoss AS 7 onwards provides a built-in CDI container. In addition to this, JBoss AS 7 also makes use of Infinispan internally for various purposes. Rather than create their own cache managers, applications deployed in JBoss AS 7 can make use of the Infinispan cache manager already created and used by JBoss AS 7, to create more cache instances for application-specific use.

The cache manager is maintained as a JBoss AS 7 resource and can be accessed using the `@Resource` annotation:

```
import javax.annotation.Resource;

public class Config {
    @Produces
    @ApplicationScoped
    @Resource
      (lookup="java:jboss/infinispan/my-container-name")
    private EmbeddedCacheManager defaultCacheManager;
}
```

Summary

In this chapter, we discussed how you could make use of Infinispan's CDI module to reduce boilerplate code, to make your code more readable and testable, and in general, improve productivity. This does require that your application is written using the CDI programming model and general guidelines.

In the next chapter, we will look at some advanced concepts in Infinispan: the Asynchronous API, the Querying API, and customizing Infinispan.

7
Advanced Topics

This chapter discusses three of Infinispan's advanced topics that go beyond simple storage and retrieval of data, configuration, and transactional characteristics:

- The asynchronous API
- The query API
- Customizing Infinispan

The asynchronous API

As powerful as Infinispan's primary API is, it is limiting in that it is designed to work equally well in both standalone and clustered modes; as a single VM object cache as well as a distributed data grid. However, to achieve this with a single API would mean giving up some of the optimizations that may be possible if assumptions around the mode of operation are allowed to influence the API.

The asynchronous API attempts to address some of this and is specific to a clustered mode of operation, as a distributed data grid.

When running Infinispan in a clustered mode, the single most expensive component of any storage or retrieval task is performing operations across a network to maintain consistency across the cluster.

Often, this performance penalty is avoided by configuring an asynchronous transport. But to do this, is to sacrifice guarantees that write operations have succeeded across a potentially unreliable network, since your application would never know if a write failed to propagate.

The asynchronous API addresses this by providing non-blocking counterparts to all `put`, `get`, and `remove` methods. These counterparts return parameterized `Future` instances instead of the results of their counterpart blocking methods. This allows the application developer to choose when to poll for the result.

As an example, the `org.infinispan.Cache` interface offers the following `put` method and its asynchronous counterpart:

```
public interface Cache<K, V> {
    ...
    V put(K key, V value);
    Future<V> putAsync(K key, V value);
    ...
}
```

The second form of the method returns before performing any network calls (and associated serialization of keys for transmission across the network), allowing the application thread to proceed with other work and check the status of the `put` method at a later point in time.

One such use of this call is to parallelize multiple writes:

```
Future<?> f1 = cache.putAsync(k1, v1);
Future<?> f2 = cache.putAsync(k2, v2);
Future<?> f3 = cache.putAsync(k3, v3);
try {
   for (Future<?> f: Arrays.asList(f1, f2, f3)) f.get();
} catch (Exception e) {
   // One of my puts failed!!
}
```

This powerful pattern allows the three writes to happen in parallel, while still maintaining synchronous guarantees. In terms of absolute performance, a lot can be gained, especially if the three keys map to different nodes in the cluster, and the actual storage operations happen in parallel.

Note: Since the actual `put` method calls, in the preceding example, happen on a different thread, one must be careful not to change the key or value passed in, until `Future` completes. Mutating either of the parameters passed in to an `async` method can result in unpredictable results.

NotifyingFuture

One would notice that the asynchronous API doesn't return a simple JDK `Future` interface. Instead, an Infinispan-specific sub-interface called `NotifyingFuture` is returned. This powerful variant of a `Future` allows the application developer to register a callback, and be notified when the `Future` completes. This allows for a more fluid program flow and saves the application developer polling the `Future` for completion status:

```
final String key = "some key";
NotifyingFuture<String> future = c.removeAsync(key);
future.attachListener(new FutureListener<String>() {
        @Override
        public void futureDone(Future<String> future) {
            try {
              future.get();
              System.out.printf
                ("The entry stored under key %s has been removed.",
                key);
            }catch (ExecutionException e) {
              System.out.printf("Failed to remove %s!", key);
            }
        }
      });
```

What happens in the preceding code is simple. A `NotifyingFuture` sub-interface is returned by the asynchronous API call. An implementation of `FutureListener` is then attached to `NotifyingFuture`. The `futureDone()` method of `FutureListener` is called when the `Future` has completed. If the `Future` has already completed when the `FutureListener` is registered, then `futureDone()` is called immediately.

In conclusion, the asynchronous API is a powerful variant to Infinispan's primary API, especially when used in clustered mode. When used properly, greater utilization of multi-core CPU architectures and network bandwidth can be realized.

The query API

When used as a distributed data grid and a NoSQL store, it is often necessary to be able to query the entire stored dataset for specific items. Keys may not always be known to an application, but different parts of a value may be queried upon. Ad hoc queries too may be required by an application.

To achieve this, Infinispan stands on the shoulders of two other open source giants: Apache Lucene, the popular document indexing and search engine, and Hibernate Search, a popular toolkit that "dehydrates" Java objects into a document-like format, which Lucene can then index and perform queries on.

Infinispan's query module indexes keys and values annotated with Hibernate Search's indexing annotations, as they are stored in Infinispan, and then updates a Lucene-based index accordingly.

Infinispan exposes a querying API that allows users to write queries using either Lucene's object-oriented query API or Hibernate Search's compatible, but much simpler and far more usable and fluent, query builder API. Once a query is created using either of these techniques, the query is passed in to the `SearchManager` interface, which then presents a user with a `CacheQuery` instance. `CacheQuery` can be lazy—lazily loading values from across a network as it is iterated over—or eager, where all results are loaded before returning the `CacheQuery` instance to the user.

Setting up your project to use Infinispan's querying capabilities

You first need to include `infinispan-query` as a dependency in your Maven `pom.xml` file:

```
<dependencies>
    ...
    <dependency>
        <groupId>org.infinispan</groupId>
        <artifactId>infinispan-query</artifactId>
        <version>${version.infinispan}</version>
    </dependency>
    ...
</dependencies>
```

If you are not using Maven, the `infinispan-query` JAR file and its dependencies are included in the zip distribution, under `modules/query`.

Configuring your cache

You also need to configure your cache to enable indexing of entries. This is done using the `<indexing>` XML element in your Infinispan configuration:

```
<?xml version="1.0" encoding="UTF-8"?>
<infinispan xmlns:xsi="http://www.w3.org/2001/XMLSchema-instance"
```

```
    xsi:schemaLocation="urn:infinispan:config:5.1 http://www.
    infinispan.org/schemas/infinispan-config-5.1.xsd"
    xmlns="urn:infinispan:config:5.1">
    <default>
     <indexing enabled="false" />
    </default>
    <namedCache name="replicated">
        <clustering mode="replicated" />
     <indexing enabled="true" indexLocalOnly="false" />
    </namedCache>
    <namedCache name="distributed">
       <clustering mode="distributed" />
     <indexing enabled="true" indexLocalOnly="true" />
    </namedCache>
</infinispan>
```

This configuration file enables indexing for two of the named caches, but not the default cache. You can also configure indexing programmatically:

```
ConfigurationBuilder builder = new ConfigurationBuilder();
builder.indexing()
      .enable()
          .indexLocalOnly(true);
Configuration cfg = builder.build();
```

NOTE: Enabling indexing and not having the appropriate `infinispan-query` JAR files on your application classpath will result in a `ConfigurationException` error.

Annotating your objects

In addition to enabling indexing, you also need to annotate your custom objects being stored in Infinispan with appropriate Hibernate Search annotations.

NOTE: There is a lot of customization and tuning that can be done with regards to how Hibernate Search indexes your objects, but that is out of the scope of this book. The excellent Hibernate Search in Action provides more information, as does Hibernate Search's online documentation at `http://search.hibernate.org`.

As a bare minimum, you need to annotate the objects you want indexed, with `@Entity`, `@Indexed`, and `@ProvidedId` and the fields within your object that you expect to search, with `@Field`.

For example:

```
@Entity @ProvidedId @Indexed
public class Person
  implements Serializable {
    @Field(store = Store.YES)
    private String name;
    @Field(store = Store.YES)
    private String description;
    @Field(store = Store.YES)
    private int age;
...
}
```

Writing a query

Let's assume that you have annotated your `Person` object as shown in the preceding code. Let's also assume that several of these have been stored in Infinispan. Searching for them is a simple matter of doing the following:

```
SearchManager manager =
  Search.getSearchManager(cache);
QueryBuilder builder =
  sm.buildQueryBuilderForClass(Person.class).get();
Query luceneQuery = builder.keyword()
            .onField("name")
            .matching("Manik")
        .createQuery();
```

This code creates a `SearchManager` and `QueryBuilder` intance, and uses these two to construct a Lucene query:

```
CacheQuery queryResult = manager.getQuery(luceneQuery);
```

The preceding code now passes this Lucene query to the `SearchManager`, to obtain a `CacheQuery` instance.

```
queryResult.list();

// Iterate over results!
for (Object result: queryResult) System.out.println("Found " +
result);
```

This `CacheQuery` instance—which contains the results to our query—can be converted into a list, can be iterated over, and so on.

Storing indexes

As mentioned, Lucene is used to store and manage indexes. Lucene itself is very configurable and comes with several different index storage subsystems, called Directories. Lucene ships with directories for simple, in-memory storage, file system storage, or storage to a relational database using JDBC. Configuring this is a matter of passing in the appropriate properties when enabling indexing in your Infinispan configuration:

```
<namedCache name="indexesInMemory">
    <indexing enabled="true">
        <properties>
            <property name=
              "hibernate.search.default.directory_provider"
              value="ram" />
        </properties>
    </indexing>
</namedCache>

<namedCache name="indexesOnDisk">
    <indexing enabled="true">
        <properties>
            <property name=
              "hibernate.search.default.directory_provider"
              value="filesystem" />
        </properties>
    </indexing>
</namedCache>
```

This example demonstrates using an in-memory, RAM-based index store for the first named cache, and a disk-based index store for the second named cache.

Infinispan directory

In addition to the default directory implementations Lucene ships with, there is also an `infinispan-directory` module, which allows Lucene to store indexes within Infinispan's distributed grid:

```
<namedCache name="indexesInInfinispan">
    <indexing enabled="true">
        <properties>
```

```
                <property name=
                  "hibernate.search.default.directory_provider"
                  value="infinispan" />
            </properties>
        </indexing>
    </namedCache>
```

In the preceding example, the named cache stores indexes back in Infinispan. This allows the indexes to be distributed, stored in-memory for fast access, and optionally written through to disk using a cache store for durability.

Index storage and cache modes

There are two strategies for storing indexes—either each node can maintain its own copy of the global index, or the index can be shared across all nodes.

Local copy of global indexes

This approach allows each node to maintain its own index and allows the use of Lucene's in-memory or filesystem-based index directory. This is only supported if your Infinispan cluster is running in replicated mode, as each node needs to be aware of each and every change to be able to keep its indexes updated. Also, when enabling indexing, the `indexLocalOnly` attribute of the `indexing` element should be set to `false`, so that even changes originating from elsewhere in the cluster are indexed:

```
<namedCache name="localCopyOfGlobalIndexes">
    <clustering mode="replicated" />
    <indexing enabled="true" indexLocalOnly="false">
      <property name=
        "hibernate.search.default.directory_provider"
        value="ram" />
    </indexing>
</namedCache>
```

Global, shared indexes

This approach relies on a single set of indexes shared by all nodes. As such, the only supported Lucene directories in this mode are the JDBC directory provider and the Infinispan directory provider, where indexes can be safely made available to the entire cluster.

Both replicated and distributed clustering modes may be used, however the `indexLocalOnly` attribute of the `indexing` element must be set to `true`, as shown here:

```
<namedCache name="globalSharedIndexes">
    <clustering mode="distributed" />
    <indexing enabled="true" indexLocalOnly="true">
      <property name=
        "hibernate.search.default.directory_provider"
        value="infinispan" />
    </indexing>
</namedCache>
```

Customizing Infinispan

Infinispan's core architecture follows the popular and well-understood Interceptor and Command/Visitor design patterns. This makes it easy to customize behavior by injecting custom interceptors to intercept API method calls.

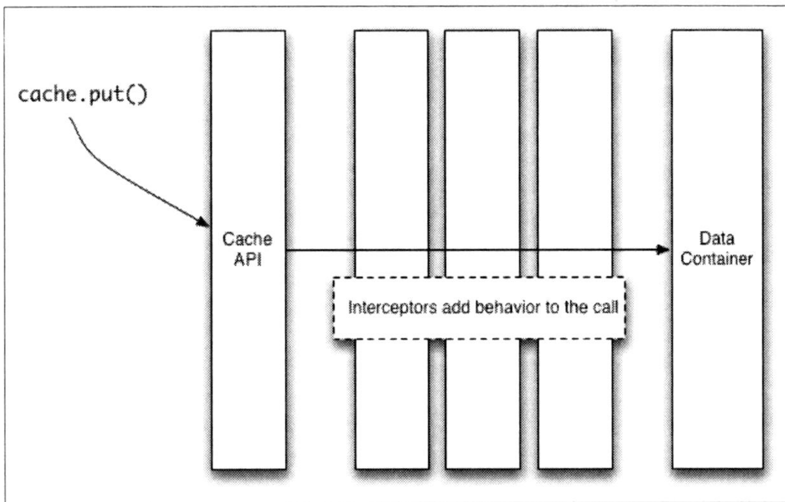

The preceding diagram demonstrates how, when calling the `put()` method on the cache, the invocation gets passed through a chain of interceptors, each one adding behavior, before `put` is finally applied to the data container that actually holds the cache entries.

Some examples of some interceptors used by Infinispan are `LockingInterceptor`, for maintaining concurrency across threads, `ReplicationInterceptor`, to ensure clustered caches are kept consistent, and `CacheStoreInterceptor`, to perform writing through to a cache store. Please see the Infinispan API documentation for a more comprehensive list of interceptors.

BaseCustomInterceptor

The `BaseCustomInterceptor` abstract class is your primary extension point. Extending this interceptor allows you to write custom interceptors and set up Infinispan to make use of your custom interceptor.

Custom interceptors can add or alter the way Infinispan behaves when certain operations are invoked:

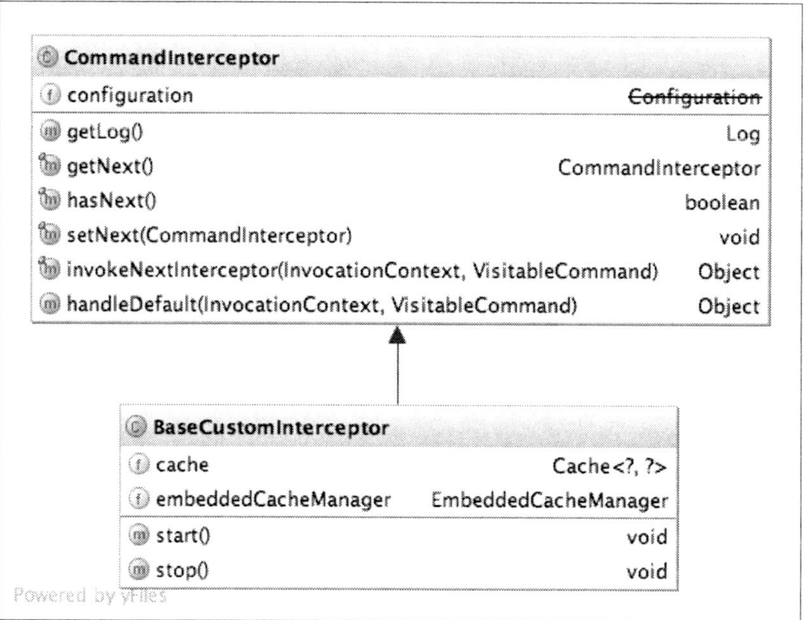

This UML class diagram depicts what fields and methods are exposed by `BaseCustomInterceptor` (as well as `CommandInterceptor`, which it extends).

`BaseCustomInterceptor` declares protected `start()` and `stop()` methods, which can be overridden if you are interested in being notified when the cache starts and stops. This allows you to perform any initialization or cleanup work in your interceptor.

It exposes protected fields referencing `Cache` and `EmbeddedCacheManager`, which provide the necessary context for your customizations.

It exposes various visitor methods, as it implements `org.infinispan.commands.Visitor`:

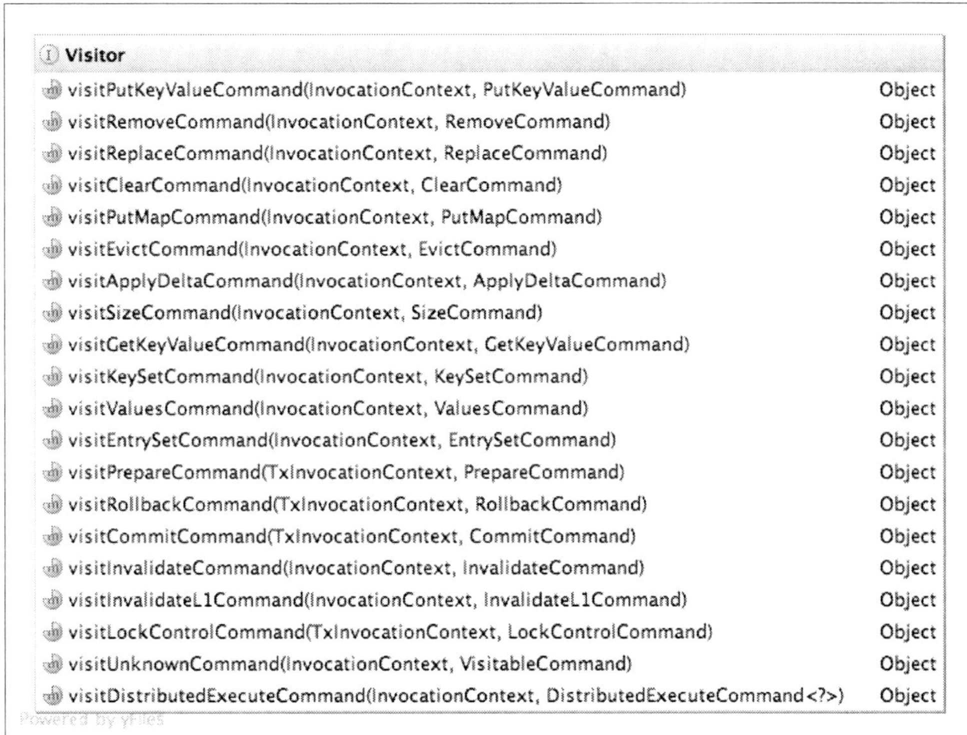

This UML class diagram depicts the method signatures defined on the **Visitor** interface. Each of these methods pertains to a different operation on the cache.

Overriding the various `visitXXX()` methods, such as `visitGetKeyValueCommand()`, allows you to intercept a `Cache.get()` operation. Note that there is also the `handleDefault()` method on `AbstractVisitor`, that can be overridden. This allows you to change the way all commands are handled. The default implementation of `handleDefault()` in `BaseCustomInterceptor` simply passes the command up the interceptor chain.

Any `visitXXX()` method or the default visitor of your custom interceptor should call `invokeNextInterceptor()` to make sure the command is passed on to the next set of interceptors to allow Infinispan to continue its work.

Commands and InvocationContext

Visitor methods take two parameters - an InvocationContext instance as well as a specific Command instance. InvocationContext contains information about the invocation, including access to the key and value affected, whether the call is of remote origin, and whether the call is transactional.

The Command instance is the encapsulation of the logic to be performed. For example, a PutKeyValueCommand instance, which is a type of Command, contains the logic needed to store an entry in the data container - the logic behind invoking put on the cache. The Command instance also contains information on whether the command has been performed, and if so, whether it was successful.

Creating a custom interceptor

Let us create a custom interceptor that causes the cache to behave in a read-only mode. This interceptor allows operations that read data, but disallows operations that update data:

```
package com.packtpub.infinispan.chapter7;

import org.infinispan.commands.write.ClearCommand;
import org.infinispan.commands.write.PutKeyValueCommand;
import org.infinispan.commands.write.PutMapCommand;
import org.infinispan.commands.write.RemoveCommand;
import org.infinispan.commands.write.ReplaceCommand;
import org.infinispan.context.InvocationContext;
import org.infinispan.interceptors.base.BaseCustomInterceptor;
import org.infinispan.util.logging.Log;
import org.infinispan.util.logging.LogFactory;

public class ReadOnlyInterceptor
  extends BaseCustomInterceptor {

    private static final Log LOG =
      LogFactory.getLog(ReadOnlyInterceptor.class);

    @Override
    protected Log getLog() {
      return LOG;
    }

    @Override
    public Object visitPutKeyValueCommand
      (InvocationContext ctx, PutKeyValueCommand cmd) {
```

```
        LOG.debug("Ignoring this call to enforce read-only behavior");
        return null;
      }

      @Override
      public Object visitPutMapCommand
        (InvocationContext ctx, PutMapCommand cmd) {
        LOG.debug("Ignoring this call to enforce read-only behavior");
        return null;
      }

      @Override
      public Object visitRemoveCommand
        (InvocationContext ctx, RemoveCommand cmd) {
        LOG.debug("Ignoring this call to enforce read-only behavior");
        return null;
     }

      @Override
      public Object visitReplaceCommand
        (InvocationContext ctx, ReplaceCommand cmd) {
        LOG.debug("Ignoring this call to enforce read-only behavior");
        return null;
      }

      @Override
      public Object visitClearCommand
        (InvocationContext ctx, ClearCommand cmd) throws Throwable {
        LOG.debug("Read-only, but we will allow the cache to be
  cleared!");
        Object o = invokeNextInterceptor(ctx, cmd);
        if (cmd.isSuccessful())
          LOG.debug("Successfully cleared the cache!")
        else
          LOG.debug("Failed to clear the cache!")
        return o;
      }
  }
```

In the previous code snippet, you can see that certain operations—such as a `put` operation or a `remove` operation—are intercepted. Rather than passing the call up the interceptor chain by calling `invokeNextInterceptor()`, these operations are logged and not passed up the chain so they do not actually do anything. All other operations, though, get passed up the chain by default and are hence unaffected by this interceptor.

Take special note of the `visitClearCommand()` method. Here, we allow clearing of the cache by allowing the command to progress up the interceptor chain, and based on the status of the command after progressing up the chain, we print an appropriate log message.

Configuring custom interceptors

Configuring custom interceptors can be done in one of two ways—either programmatically or declaratively. Starting with programmatic configuration, we have the following:

```
ConfigurationBuilder builder =
  new ConfigurationBuilder();
  builder.customInterceptors()
        .addInterceptor()
          .interceptor(new ReadOnlyInterceptor())
          .position(InterceptorConfiguration.Position.FIRST);
  Configuration c = builder.build();
```

This code snippet adds your new interceptor to the configuration, as the first interceptor in the chain. To do the same thing declaratively, using XML, use the following code snippet:

```
<?xml version="1.0" encoding="UTF-8"?>
<infinispan
    xmlns:xsi=
      "http://www.w3.org/2001/XMLSchema-instance"
    xsi:schemaLocation=
      "urn:infinispan:config:5.1
      http://www.infinispan.org/schemas/infinispan-config-5.1.xsd"
    xmlns="urn:infinispan:config:5.1">

    <global />

    <default />

    <namedCache name="cacheWithCustomInterceptor">
      <customInterceptors>
        <interceptor class=
          "com.packtpub.infinispan.chapter7.ReadOnlyInterceptor"
          position="FIRST" />
      </customInterceptors>
    </namedCache>

</infinispan>
```

Interceptor positioning

There is a certain amount of flexibility in how you control where your custom interceptor is placed in the interceptor chain. It can be immediately before or after a specified interceptor type, using the `before` or `after` attributes to the `customInterceptors` XML tag.

You could alternatively use an index (0 being the first position); however, using an index can be dangerous as you could be exposed to an index being out of bounds. This is represented by the `index` XML attribute.

The third and safest way to define the position of the interceptor is to use the `position` attribute, which takes in ordinals such as `FIRST`, `LAST`, or `OTHER_THAN_FIRST_OR_LAST`. Use the `position` XML attribute for this.

Summary

In this chapter, we covered three advanced topics related to Infinispan.

The powerful asynchronous API gives you the ability to parallelize your remote writes, while still receiving feedback on the success of such remote writes.

The query API allows you to index the data you store in Infinispan and write queries against it.

We then finally covered how to extend Infinispan by making use of custom interceptors to add or modify Infinispan's behavior.

Index

Symbols

A

B

C

D

E

F

G

H

I

U

V

W

Thank you for buying
Infinispan Data Grid Platform

About Packt Publishing

Packt, pronounced 'packed', published its first book "*Mastering phpMyAdmin for Effective MySQL Management*" in April 2004 and subsequently continued to specialize in publishing highly focused books on specific technologies and solutions.

Our books and publications share the experiences of your fellow IT professionals in adapting and customizing today's systems, applications, and frameworks. Our solution based books give you the knowledge and power to customize the software and technologies you're using to get the job done. Packt books are more specific and less general than the IT books you have seen in the past. Our unique business model allows us to bring you more focused information, giving you more of what you need to know, and less of what you don't.

Packt is a modern, yet unique publishing company, which focuses on producing quality, cutting-edge books for communities of developers, administrators, and newbies alike. For more information, please visit our website: `www.packtpub.com`.

About Packt Open Source

In 2010, Packt launched two new brands, Packt Open Source and Packt Enterprise, in order to continue its focus on specialization. This book is part of the Packt Open Source brand, home to books published on software built around Open Source licences, and offering information to anybody from advanced developers to budding web designers. The Open Source brand also runs Packt's Open Source Royalty Scheme, by which Packt gives a royalty to each Open Source project about whose software a book is sold.

Writing for Packt

We welcome all inquiries from people who are interested in authoring. Book proposals should be sent to author@packtpub.com. If your book idea is still at an early stage and you would like to discuss it first before writing a formal book proposal, contact us; one of our commissioning editors will get in touch with you.

We're not just looking for published authors; if you have strong technical skills but no writing experience, our experienced editors can help you develop a writing career, or simply get some additional reward for your expertise.

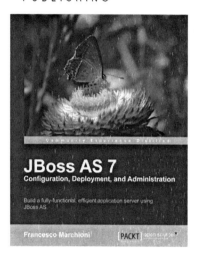

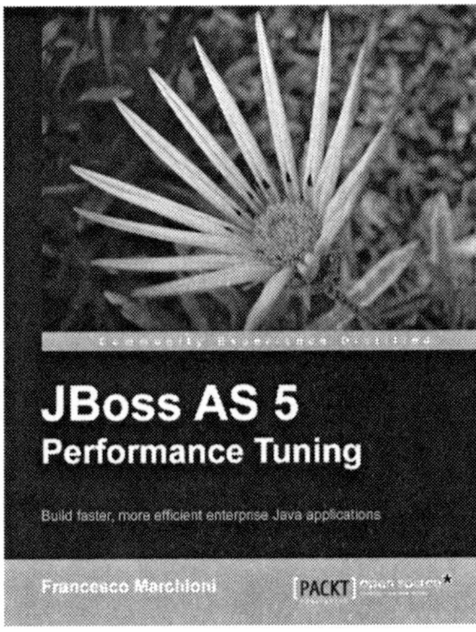

JBoss AS 5 Performance Tuning

ISBN: 9781849514026 Paperback: 312 pages

Build faster, more efficient enterprise Java applications

1. Follow the practical examples to make your applications as efficient as possible
2. Written to version 5.1 and includes advice on upgrading to version 6.0
3. Accurately configure the persistence layer and clustering service
4. Learn how to tune all components and hardware

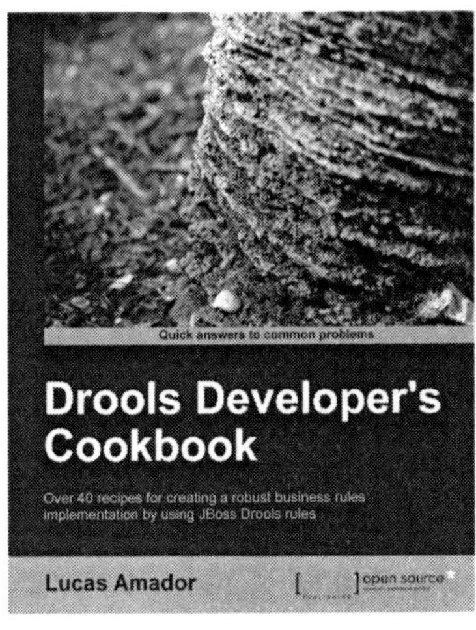

Drools Developer's Cookbook

ISBN: 9781849511964 Paperback: 310 pages

Over 40 recipes for creating a robust business rules implementation by using JBoss Drools rules

1. Master the newest Drools Expert, Fusion, Guvnor, Planner and jBPM5 features
2. Integrate Drools by using popular Java Frameworks
3. Part of Packt's Cookbook series: each recipe is independent and contains practical, step-by-step instructions to help you achieve your goal.

Please check **www.PacktPub.com** for information on our titles

CPSIA information can be obtained at www.ICGtesting.com
Printed in the USA
LVOW111745210812

295317LV00009B/9/P